STAN LEVEY

JAZZ

HEAVYWEIGHT

THE AUTHORIZED BIOGRAPHY

STAN LEVEY
JAZZ
HEAVYWEIGHT

THE AUTHORIZED BIOGRAPHY

FRANK R. HAYDE
FOREWORD BY CHARLIE WATTS

SANTA
MONICA
PRESS

Published by:

Santa Monica Press LLC
P.O. Box 850
Solana Beach, CA 92075
1-800-784-9553
www.santamonicapress.com
books@santamonicapress.com

Printed in the United States

Santa Monica Press books are available at special quantity discounts when
purchased in bulk by corporations, organizations, or groups. Please call our
Special Sales department at 1-800-784-9553.

This book is intended to provide general information. The publisher, author,
distributor, and copyright owner are not engaged in rendering professional
advice or services. The publisher, author, distributor, and copyright owner
are not liable or responsible to any person or group with respect to any loss,
illness, or injury caused or alleged to be caused by the information found in
this book.

ISBN-13 978-1-59580-086-2

Library of Congress Cataloging-in-Publication Data

Names: Hayde, Frank R.
Title: Stan Levey : jazz heavyweight / by Frank R. Hayde.
Description: Solana Beach, California : Santa Monica Press, [2016] | Includes
bibliographical references and index.
Identifiers: LCCN 2015041922 | ISBN 9781595800862
Subjects: LCSH: Levey, Stan. | Jazz musicians--United States--Biography. |
Drummers (Musicians)--United States--Biography.
Classification: LCC ML419.L447 H39 2016 | DDC 786.9/165092—dc23
LC record available at http://lccn.loc.gov/2015041922

Cover and interior design and production by Future Studio

All photos courtesy of the Stan Levey Family collection, with the exception
of page xiii, upper, © Ross Burdick/CTSIMAGES.

CONTENTS

INTRODUCTION BY **CHARLIE WATTS** OF THE ROLLING STONES 7

CHAPTER 1: **NATURAL RHYTHM**.. 9

CHAPTER 2: **THE FIGHT RACKET** 31

CHAPTER 3: **FIFTY-SECOND STREET**............................ 39

CHAPTER 4: **THE BIRD FLIES IN** 51

CHAPTER 5: **BEBOP**.. 59

CHAPTER 6: **CALIFORNIA** 71

CHAPTER 7: **PRISON AND REDEMPTION**...................... 91

CHAPTER 8: **ARTISTRY IN RHYTHM**............................. 99

CHAPTER 9: **BIRD LIVES!**....................................... 111

CHAPTER 10: **WEST COAST COOL**.................................. 117

CHAPTER 11: **THE BIG TIME**................................... 131

CHAPTER 12: **HOLLYWOOD STUDIOS** 143

CHAPTER 13: **LIFE AFTER MUSIC** 151

RECOMMENDED LISTENING 169

EPILOGUE.. 193

ACKNOWLEDGMENTS.. 212

SOURCES.. 214

INDEX.. 218

NOTE TO THE READER

This book alternates between the author's third person narrative and Stan Levey's own words, which appear in this font and feature a bold, drumstick line along the left side of the quote.

Stan's own words come from audio recordings provided by his family, and other interviews and sources listed herein. Most of Stan's quotes are verbatim, but I have linked sentences he spoke on the same subject from different sources. Direct quotes he spoke to family members, who relayed them to me, are sometimes attributed directly to Stan instead of through the person he spoke them to. In some cases, I have taken artistic license in how Stan expressed something if it served to eliminate confusion, clarify the context of the subject matter, correct errors in chronology, etc.

INTRODUCTION

by CHARLIE WATTS of the Rolling Stones

The first time I heard of Stan Levey was when I was about fifteen years old and I was collecting all the Charlie Parker stuff. The band that Dizzy Gillespie took to Los Angeles in about 1946—an *amazing* band—Stan was in that band. Stan was one of the original bebop players from this very innovative period when they completely changed playing. To hold down the drum chair with Dizzy and Parker is something else.

Stan could hold a tempo that was unbelievable. It's very difficult to play fast and keep on top of it. *Really* difficult. It takes a whole sort of athleticism. You have to jump—be on top of every beat—hold a tempo on top of a tempo. Stan was a master of that. The other thing with Stan is he was a very good boxer. That's what I think kept him in great shape for that sort of thing.

He moved to Hollywood and was playing what's called West Coast jazz. Those are my favorite records of Stan, that stuff from Contemporary Records, which had a yellow record label, and Bethlehem Records. For me as a young sixteen- or eighteen-year-old in London, buying records and trying to learn how to play, Stan was synonymous with the West Coast school. To see them all playing live, these jazz musicians in the 1950s, must have been unbelievably fantastic. One of the bands Stan played in that gave him terrific notoriety was the Stan Kenton band.

I think this is a piece of jazz history that's very important to document. Stan is a link. His life is an amazing story and he was a lovely man. I was totally in awe of meeting him and the legacy that he carries.

CHAPTER I

NATURAL RHYTHM

No toys in young Stan Levey's room—only a bed, a closet, a little bureau, and a big, lonely boy. The only sound was his clock: the wind-up kind with crisp precision time, loud and percussive.

❢ I could hear it all the way from the bathroom.

Sometimes he'd save a picture of a toy from a newspaper or magazine—Lincoln Logs or an erector set. The pictures were a sad substitute, and when their novelty wore off, it was back to the clock.

Stan's father was a boxing manager and part owner of a used car lot. As a fight manager in 1930s and '40s Philadelphia, he occupied a low-level position in the national crime syndicate. Stan's mother Esther, known to all as Essie, was a comely and intelligent woman with domestic skills, style, and musical talent, but she was an alcoholic.

❢ It didn't take much to affect her. A drink or two and *pow!* She was slurring her words and staggering.

Though he was born Adolph Stan Levey, Stan's parents always called him by his middle name. He didn't have any

brothers or sisters. When his parents fought and screamed and
drank, he'd focus on the rhythm of the clock.

> I'd take a couple of pencils and improvise beats between the
> clock's ticking: *One-two-three, one-two-three, FOUR!*
>
> I was obsessed with rhythm. I'd tap my spoon and fork
> on a glass of milk or a dinner plate or the edge of the table.
> That would push Dave over the top. I never called him "dad"
> or "pop," or even "father." It was "Dave" as far back as I can
> remember.
>
> "Stop your goddamn drumming on the table!"
>
> My mother took my side when Dave was home.
>
> "Well, Dave Levey, if you'd buy him a drum set, he
> wouldn't take it out on the table!"
>
> "You know how much a drum set costs?"

Their fighting was frequent and intense and usually ended
the same way, with Dave withdrawing into his angry, silent
self, and Stan's mother secretly taking another drink.

For eight or nine years, they lived on Lindley Avenue off
Broad Street, a lower-middle-class neighborhood in North
Philadelphia. Their apartment building looked like all the
others on the quiet, tree-lined street. In good weather, Stan
would play a little stickball or half-ball with three or four of
the neighborhood boys.

Cockroaches plagued every house on the block, but the
Leveys' small apartment was always clean. Essie was a diligent
housekeeper. She was also a tasty cook, specializing in the stew
recipes her mother brought with her from Lithuania. The lino-
leum-floored kitchen had a small, early model refrigerator with
the coil on top. Every Sunday, Essie would dress up the dining
area with a white tablecloth and serve homemade fried chicken.

The living room offered a touch of elegance in the form of a baby grand piano that Stan's musically endowed mother could play by ear, if only in one key. Her tastes bordered on the sophisticated, with a wide-eyed admiration for Art Tatum. Nearby stood the radio, an old Majestic model that Stan loved to listen to when his parents weren't using the room to argue. His favorite band was the Clicquot Club Eskimos from *The Adventures of Ozzie and Harriet.*

I wait for that every Sunday, boy, my hands, wrists, arms moving to the swing beats. Traditional 4/4s, *ratta-tatta, ratta-tatta.*

Ever encouraging of Stan's musical instincts, Essie brought home a used record player and a new record by trumpeter Erskine Hawkins. Stan's father was not impressed.

"My old man used to call him 'Irksome' Hawkins," said Stan.

At Essie's urging, Stan's father took his ten-year-old son to see Chick Webb at the Earle Theater. It was an electrifying event for the little boy, one he would remember vividly for the rest of his life.

Chick Webb was a hunchback who stood less than five feet tall. But the smallest man in jazz was a monster on the drums and the undisputed champion of the legendary big band battles, where competing orchestras set up on opposite ends of the bandstand and traded sets like counterpunches. The events were marketed like boxing matches and the stakes were just as high. A victory was as valuable to a bandleader's career as a main event was to a boxer's. The winner was generally the band that whipped the dancers into the most ecstatic frenzy of the night.

The Savoy Ballroom in Harlem was the Madison Square Garden of big band "boxing," and Chick Webb defended his title from there, welcoming all challengers. The *Amsterdam News* described one of Chick Webb's battles with Count Basie in this way:

> Throughout the fight, which never let down in its intensity during the whole fray, Chick took the aggressive, with Count playing along easily and . . . more musically, scientifically. Undismayed by Chick's forceful drum beating, which sent the audience into shouts of encouragement and appreciation and caused beads of perspiration to drop from Chick's brow onto the brass cymbals, the Count maintained an attitude of poise and self-assurance. He . . . parried Chick's thundering haymakers with tantalizing runs and arpeggios which teased more and more force from his adversary.

Webb's epic battle with Benny Goodman required mounted police to manage the thousands who couldn't get inside the overflowing ballroom. Chick gave Benny a beating that night. Goodman's drummer, Gene Krupa, said that Chick had "cut me to ribbons."

Stan didn't know that Webb was a hunchback and was initially confused and astonished at what he was seeing, let alone what he was hearing. Webb's drumming was a complete departure from anything he'd heard before. Stan was mesmerized, but not too much to notice the singer, a teenage Ella Fitzgerald. Little did Stan know that thirty years later she'd have him in her band—one of the most coveted and best-paying jobs in jazz.

But Stan's life after seeing Chick Webb went right back to the alternating screams and silences of his family's small apartment, which was penetrated only by Stan's extended family.

I guess I'm Jewish, though religion sure isn't a big deal in our house. Dave's parents are Russian. Bessie and Herman. Herman is five feet tall and five feet wide with a big cigar—a character. My grandmother Bessie won't let me call her Grandma. I have to call her "Aunt Bess." They live close to us. And I meet my grandfather's parents—they've just come over from Russia. I don't know their names. They look like two little birds and their eyes are watering. I've never seen anybody that old and frail and it actually scares me. They die soon after.

Herman's always tapped out for money. He owns the used car lot with my old man and he's an inventor. Of course nothing ever works out for him, like this thing he comes up with to keep the beer moving. It has coils, so the beer would come up—keep it from getting flat. It doesn't work.

Aunt Bess is big, strong, very blustering, very outgoing. Herman is beat down. She beats him up mentally. My father has two sisters who kind of disappeared. My mother has a sister and her husband. He's in the automobile business and they're struggling like us—just working people. They live right above us. Their son is Lenny, my first cousin, two years younger. He isn't athletic, and we just do stuff like the string on the can, talking to each other. He tries to play the clarinet, but nothing comes of it.

Also on my mom's side is Grandma Hoffman, a wonderful woman. Hates the fact that her daughter drinks, loves me and Lenny. Wonderful cook. Always cheerful. Lithuanian—speaks with an accent. She has her own hotel in Atlantic City, the Baronet, and she always gives my father money

'cause he's always short. She's the one person I can really relate to. She cooks for the whole hotel, about twenty
rooms. Whatever she makes is good. She has an icebox,
with the ice delivered. She makes everything, all the Jewish
cooking— goulash, chicken. She cooks three meals a day for
that whole hotel, maybe thirty, thirty-five people. And she
makes cinnamon buns, man—best you ever ate. Heavy, very
angelic face, good teeth, but she's worn out from taking care
of this hotel, cooking three meals a day. Her husband had
died. Never met him. In the summertime she has me and my
mother down. My father comes on the weekend. Lay on the
beach. It's great.

My mother's a pretty woman, intelligent, tall, elegant,
well-spoken. I'd show her off anywhere, if it wasn't for the
liquor. There's those times she's loud or belligerent or slop-
py—shoes come off, hair mussed up, yells at Dave, swings at
me, throws things, breaking, swearing—that's when I know
I love her but she'll never do anything outside the house but
embarrass me.

She has a friend he doesn't like, Edna, and her husband,
his name is Abe, he has money. And she's a drinker, comes
over at three in the afternoon and starts whacking it down
and they get swacked. Funny thing is, I never see her take a
drink, not a drop. I don't know how much she goes through
in a day.

Then he comes home. He's always very tired. My old man
was very quiet and did a lot of grunting. Cigar, you know.
Comes home from selling used cars and she's drunk, passed
out on the sofa, and he starts screaming, "Why I gotta come
home to this crap!" I go into my room. I don't want to hear
it. Screaming, things breaking.

Brought my buddy David over. Everybody knows about

that family. He's a lunatic; abuses his parents, pushes them around. That's what I like—a rebel. He's in charge. They're the children, he's the parent. Nine years old, David's already nuts, really crazy. Abuses his parents, knocks his parents around, rearranges the furniture in his house. I like him. Does all the decorating; puffs the pillows up, moves the furniture into the middle of the room. Father's a little insurance guy that goes around with his book and takes a dollar here, a quarter here, and plays the violin. A nutcake, too. And the mother's nutty. But he's my friend. The decorator of his house and they just stand there. They try to do something— he goes into a rage. I'm forbidden to play with him cause my parents know right away he's crazy. My only friend: Gone.

Dave never says a word to me, even our Sunday fried chicken dinners with the tablecloth are silent. Until she utters something, and he tells her, "You're drunk!" Dave doesn't drink. The man can eat though. He can eat, I tell ya. Nice, little napkins at that table, but no talking. He just eats.

Dave's dream is to get rich. He has a stable of sixteen fighters, some rough, some mean, some just good, hard-working men, but all of them look like dollar signs to Dave. He buys or sells them at the drop of a hat. Whatever will put more cash in his pocket. You don't want to buy a car from him.

As the son of a manager, Stan had opportunities to hang around the gym and step into the ring, but it was his size and strength that allowed him to break into professional boxing while he was still a teenager. Six-foot-two Levey qualified as a heavyweight in the 1940s. Though he weighed only a hundred and seventy-eight pounds, Stan's leanness was deceiving. He had hands like catcher's mitts and a heavy jaw anchored by a brick of a chin, which looked specifically designed to take a punch. Throughout his life, the hulking drummer gave off an impression of hugeness that was universally intimidating. Stan's wife Angela recalled an inside joke that Stan was from the ape family. "He'd see an orangutan on television and say, 'Oh, look, it's my uncle Abe,'" said Angela, "'and there's my brother the chimp.'"

But young Stan also had another pugilistic attribute. Like so many other boxers, he had learned to take a beating early, at home.

Like every other kid in Philly and the world, I always pretend to be sick to stay away from school, but this one morning, she's got half a load on already, and she says, "Get the hell out of here," and *bam*—a belt with a big buckle. Whacks me. Opens my head up big time. I'm maybe seven, so she calls the doctor. Two-dollar doctor, comes to the house for two bucks. She gets nervous. "Tell him . . . tell him you fell down."

He says, "What happened?"

She says, "Oh, he fell, he fell," and I say, "Yeah, I fell." It's a good whack.

The old man, he's like a gorilla. That's where I got these long arms, these shoulders. He's bald and hairy. Big arms. Takes me down to the basement and says, "You're gonna learn to box!"

Now, I'm really young—nine, ten. I'm saying, "This is great, man, I'm getting attention." We start pummeling. He starts laying right into me. He hurts me, but I enjoy it. Stomach, face . . . beats the hell out of me, but I enjoy it. Then I start to lay back into him and he doesn't like that. He hits harder. We have a coal chute down there. The truck puts that chute down through the window and the coal comes down for the furnace. Big empty place, coal dust in the air. Breathing it. He's beating the shit out of me. Says, "Come here, I want to show you a couple things." I say, "Yeah, great, he's talkin' to me!"

He drops it like a bomb at dinner one night: "We're going to the fights!" First time, very exciting. Thursday night fights. I'm maybe nine. Down on Broad—the Olympic Fight Club—South Broad Street, at night. School doesn't matter at all. My mom maybe worries about my grades a couple of times, but it passes. Him? Never.

Takes me right back to the dressing room. They're taping up and he introduces me to a couple of his guys. It's a thrill to be there. I'm saying, "Wow, look at these guys, they're gonna go in and *fight*!"

The Olympic holds maybe three hundred. Smoky, man— the whole place stinks just awful. All the beat-up ex-fighters selling peanuts. We get peanuts. Ring announcer's a little guy—shirt and bow tie, high voice, no microphone—introduces the fighters, kind of nasal, high-toned, piercing voice so it projects, cuts through. They bet the white corner or the black corner. Bet on the round, the knockout. The lights dim and these two guys come out. Our guys are later.

I'll do anything to gain his attention, my old man. That's why I become a boxer. He takes me down to the gym, where all his boxers are. Right away they like me and I start working out with them. I'm a big kid. First time I must've been twelve or thirteen. Eventually, I'm working out with Bob Montgomery and Ike Williams—world champions— not really realizing how important they are at that particular time. But that's to get my old man's attention when I go in and start boxing. He doesn't even come around, just takes me and shows me off.

"That's my boy. Look how big he is."

"Yeah, he's a big kid, Dave. Big, strong kid."

But once we leave, it's not a word. Zip.

Stan got his first drum set a couple of years before he started working out at the gym. He was walking past Ted Burke's Music Store with his mother, and they saw it in the window. Stan's reaction was so passionate that it moved Essie to sober up long enough to speak to Dave.

Somehow, my mother gathers herself.

"Dave. Dave, are you listening to me?"

"What the hell? You been drinking?"

"Dave, the boy's got nothing. *Nothing.*"

"Whattayamean nothing? A roof over his head? Three squares? A freaking radio for Christ's sake! What do you want from me? Leave me alone."

"David."

"Oh, now it's David! What the hell, I know you've been drinking."

"No, I haven't. Not this time. He's got nothing. Listen to me. Be a father. Buy him drums. He's got a beat, Dave, he's got rhythm."

"What? I don't have that kind of money. What are you talking about?"

"There's a little set. We saw it at Ted Burke's, a kid set, cheap. A man does this, Dave. Your son has nothing. You've never given him anything. Give him this. Be a man. Be a man, huh?"

The one Christmas this Jewish boy ever gets. Put up my little tiny gorgeous set right in front of the Majestic and let those Eskimos guide me into the music. Play along, feel my way, carried along . . .

One time! One time, I catch my folks sitting, arms around each other behind me on the old sofa, just watching me play, holding each other. Never again, but that's all it takes. I know I have something, man—something special to make them do that. That tiny bass drum, snare, cymbal, those brushes, my folks watching me like that . . . Nothing else to say. Nothing else to do.

When Stan was thirteen, his family moved into a two-story row house in West Philadelphia. On the surface, the move indicated an improvement in the family's fortune. They were still renters, but their new house was more spacious, with three bedrooms, two baths, and an outdoor patio. While their old apartment had been coal-fired and sooty, their new dwelling was powered by natural gas. Stan became friendly with the gas man, a fellow jazz lover and aspiring trombonist named Bill Harris.

But for Stan, the new house represented the end of his parents' marriage. Essie's drinking worsened and the animosity between her and Dave climaxed on the staircase one evening with Essie wielding a thirteen-inch butcher knife in a drunken rage. Dave walked out and divorce followed.

Stan started cutting school so he could study the drummers at the Earle Theater's live music matinees. Sometimes it was just the pit band, other times it was a headliner like Gene Krupa or Buddy Rich playing with Artie Shaw. Stan absorbed ideas, memorized licks, and ogled the mother-of-pearl drum kits that made his little practice set seem like a mere toy.

Stan also came to realize he'd been playing backwards, as if he were left-handed, but he made a conscious decision not to change what "felt right." For the rest of his career, Stan's

southpaw stance was a distinguishing quirk and a source of
curiosity for young drummers who studied him, just as he'd
studied the drummers at the Earle. Rumors floated that it was
a crafty offshoot of his boxing strategy, but Stan always admitted that it was simply the badge of a self-taught kid who didn't
know any better.

When Dave moved out, Stan tried to stay connected to
him through boxing. He started training in earnest and became a gofer and sometime corner man for his father's fighters.

At the gym, I'm like a little mascot, a little white mascot.
All the guys are black where I train. Spring Garden Gym—
Sixth and Gerard. There might be a hundred fighters training
there, some in the morning, some in the afternoon, some at
night. It's staggered.

Dave has this fighter, Georgie Miller—one of those great
guys—outgoing, funny, good guy. I'm fourteen, fifteen. He's
a middleweight, about one hundred and fifty-six pounds, tall,
about six feet, pretty tall for a middleweight, very dark skin,
so black it was almost purple. Great teeth, great smile, and
he has two cauliflower ears and very proud of it. He's twenty-four, twenty-five. My old man wants to have them slice
the ears and fix them. No, no, he won't have it. Who wants
to walk around with that? But that's his badge of battle, so
he leaves it. Dave wants the procedure—then it won't get
hit again and infected, whatever. Usually they cut it and it all
collapses in. But no, not Georgie.

Georgie takes to me. We just like each other. I'm training and he says, "Come on, man, step it up, faster on the
rope!" Then he shows me tricks in the ring, how to duck
and dodge, stuff like that. He'd say he'd like to go a couple of
rounds with me and teach me which is the superior race of

men. Then he'd lean down and whisper in my ear, "Hey man, we fighters got to stick together, don't we?" One time he calls me over and whispers, "Hey man, you want something real good?" I say, "Yeah, what?" He whispers, "I can get you some high-grade barbecue sauce."

He's almost like a father to me in a way. That's the feeling I get from him. I'm the boss's son, but he goes past that. He likes me for what I am. He has a protective feeling toward me, and I really like this guy. In the gym, or he comes around the used car lot. He's an older guy, he pats my shoulder. I wished I owned a set of teeth like he had. They sparkled when he smiled. He was always smiling, even when he climbed into the ring.

One night, he's the third fight on the ticket. Unless you were one of the top-liners of the night, the fighters shared a common dressing room. His opponent was a mean-looking Polish guy. He had hair all over his body. I don't remember his name. "Hey, man," Georgie says, "Catch that hairy-lookin' dude." The guy never cracked a smile or said anything. He just turned his back. Georgie's grin kind of froze. I think he realized his joking had gone too far.

The old man doesn't show up that night. I'm working the corner, buckets and all that. He can't handle the Polish guy. Just too strong for him. The referee doesn't seem to care when he butts Georgie with his head in the clinch. I think in the third round he goes down. Bleeding from everywhere. He's shot. Loses a front tooth, right in the middle of that great smile. He's beat up. Beat. In those days, they would do that, you know—a mismatch. Put one guy in with a sure winner so they knew how to bet. Never mind how bad the patsy gets beaten up.

I get all peed off at my old man.

"Man, your fighter was there! Where were you? Georgie got hurt bad. You should've been there. You should've stopped the goddamn fight. Was he set up?"

He don't talk. Who knows? All he says is, "Don't ask too many questions."

I sparred with other fighters and learned a lot dodging their fists. When I got hit it made me madder than hell, so I trained hard and was in top condition. Dave came around the gym and watched but he never gave me encouragement or even a smile.

Surprisingly, I'm bar mitzvahed. They get me a rabbi, he teaches me the words, I study hard because Dave promises me a party with money and presents. Says I'll become a man. The day comes and, *ah-ha*! The old man takes all the checks. I never see the money. He says, "I'm holding it for you." Well, I'm still looking for it. My mother dresses up that day. Everything was good. That's it. I'm a man.

By then, I had some friends. Met my friend Stuffy. He plays the piano, and so do I, a little from my mother. We play drums and piano for hours. Good hand-eye coordination. He has a good solid family. Mother, father who's a taskmaster. We play poker down in the basement for pennies, big win, a quarter. Stuffy's father says "Henry"—that's Stuffy's real name—"Henry, it's time to come up and study."

There's also a clarinet player, Marv Goodman, around where I live and he has a little band. Somehow we meet and he gets this little gig at the Temple Youth Club, three nights a week from five to seven, something like that. I'm a kid, about thirteen. Piano, drums, and clarinet: just a trio, three guys. We play tunes—tunes of the day. I just lock into what I'm doing. I don't see anyone out there.

When I hit the ninth grade, I dropped out. I couldn't

stand the place, the teachers, the kids. I didn't make a lot of friends like some kids do. I didn't join clubs and that type of thing. Still, some voice inside kept warning me, "Don't do it, Stan. Don't quit. You'll be sorry." What the hell? I did it anyway. Well, later in life you regret it, yeah. I would've liked to have an education. I learned mine on the street, which a lot of people did in those days, you know.

That went for music, too. There was no information anywhere. No books or videos. No records, hardly. You had to wait for a band to come in maybe twice a year, try to get a look at the drummer, see what he's doing. There's no information about how to hold sticks, or how to set up and put a drum kit together. Now every kid has a garage with a drum set. I was completely self-taught because we couldn't afford a teacher, and that's why I play left-handed although I am right-handed.

Stan went to work with his father and grandfather, washing and simonizing jalopies at the used car lot, located at Broad and Huntingdon Streets, where Dave Levey was not above putting sawdust in a crankcase—an old trick used to silence worn-out parts and keep a bad engine from smoking.

In 1942, Dave was arrested and jailed in a gambling raid. His charges were later "dismissed for lack of evidence." Working with partner Jack Hofberg and trainer Jimmy Collins, Stan's father also continued to manage a stable of fighters, including knockout specialist Johnny Walker; promising lightweights Dorsey Lay and Bob Jennings; welterweights Pedro Tomez and Leo Peterson; heavyweights Willie Thomas, Gus Jones, and Jackie Saunders; and middleweights John Finney and Newton Smith, who died tragically from blunt trauma while fighting Sam Bouradi for Dave in 1947 (eerily, Bouradi

died under similar circumstances only six months later at the
hands of Ezzard Charles). Dave lost another fighter the following year when Johnny Walker drowned in a YMCA swimming
pool in Ohio.

For Stan, the pieces fell into place for the typical dead-
end life of a dropout, but the young man waited less than a
year before setting himself on the path that would lead him
out of the used car lot and on to bigger things in life. Stan
would modestly attribute it to luck with a qualifier of ability,
but American-style ambition and some considerable chutzpa
also helped when he hitched his wagon to the fastest rising star
in the music business.

John Birks Gillespie earned the nickname "Dizzy" for
his mischievous ways and onstage antics. In the early 1940s,
he was back home in Philadelphia after a stint in New York
and a coast-to-coast tour with Cab Calloway's band, one of
the top grossing acts in show business. Dizzy Gillespie was
only twenty-five years old and not yet well-known, but he
was about to become the vanguard of a new movement and a
new paradigm of virtuosity. Stan couldn't have found a more
auspicious musician if he'd tried. One afternoon, he was walking down the street when he chanced upon Gillespie's music
wafting down from a rehearsal on the second story of the
Downbeat Club.

I'm walking down Eleventh Street in Philly and I hear this
trumpet coming through the window, in the daytime. I don't
even know they have any music in there. I hear this trumpet
and I say, "Man, it sounds like Roy Eldridge but with a left-
hand turn." The changes!

I'm hearing this guy and I think, "Wow, I gotta go up and
see what's going on up there!" And I go up these steps to this

bar, daytime, and they're rehearsing, and I just sit around the bar, listening, listening, listening. And then Dizzy comes down after they take a break and he says, "How you doin', man?" I say, "I'm a drummer too, you know." I was a little pissant.

"You're a drummer? Well, come on up and sit in."

Oh, now I've done it! So just as a gag they let me play, and I play pretty good. So I say, "I'd love to come down some night and hear you guys." He says, "Come on in, don't worry about the owner, just come on up and sit next to me."

And I do that. Go in and listen to the band, and once in a while sit in a little bit. Sometimes he shows me something, he says, "Do this, try this." Diz is a marvelous teacher. I never saw anybody that open and willing to give his knowledge to people. So encouraging—freely gives of himself to young musicians. He was loved all over the world for that.

He takes me aside and executes what he feels should accompany his music. "Did you ever hear of Shadow Wilson?" Of course, I hadn't. I've never heard of anybody. He sits down and plays something from Shadow. Diz's drum technique isn't great, but he can illustrate exactly how to do things and he's an excellent sight reader. I'm only sixteen and thrilled with our relationship. He almost forces my talent out into the open. He has so many terrific rhythmic ideas. "Salt Peanuts"—the tempo is almost impossible. Diz works out the patterns and spoon-feeds the whole thing to his drummers. After you play it for a while, it doesn't seem difficult at all.

One night Dizzy's drummer, Jerry Gilgore, says, "I've got this gig, I've got to go." And Dizzy says to Jerry, "Go ahead, man, make some money and good luck."

I don't think I'm up to it, but Dizzy says, "Well, Stan, want to try it?"

"Yeah."

Nervous, but I get through it and he likes it. He always encourages me, all through my life.

So I get the job! Eighteen dollars a week! Join the union. We play six nights a week. Oscar Smith, the bass player, is a schoolteacher, and the pianist is Johnny Acea. The owner is Nat Siegel, a clarinet player who plays in the pit band at the Earle Theater. He's a good guy. He likes Dizzy. Once in a while he plays a little clarinet—not too good, but he owns the place. Short, bad leg, dark hair, very scattered type of talk. He's okay.

Diz would keep giving me advice: "Get up in the front line. Make a statement. Play against the horns. Improvise a little. Play in a musical way." He wanted the drummer to be freer, more creative, to listen and do things to help the other players. He showed me the old ways wouldn't work with the new music. Four clops to the bar were out. Dizzy wanted the drums to punctuate, as in a paragraph, to punctuate what he was doing musically. This music was flying. It had wings.

One night she comes in—my mother—sits at the end of the bar, has a blast then splits. Of course, I'm worried about her behavior. But she leaves early. She knows I'm playing and comes in, just shows up.

Oscar Smith, Dizzy's bassist schoolteacher, remembered Stan as "a white guy who played well and sort of passed for black." Stan's time in the Spring Garden Gym had apparently acculturated him well for his entry into the African-American art form of jazz. His job with Dizzy boosted his confidence and gave him a taste of his own earning power.

When he turned seventeen, Stan lied about his age to the

boxing commission and started casting about for his first paying fight.

But even before that, another seemingly impossible musical opportunity opened up for young Stan. Shortly after joining up with Dizzy, the teenager was invited to play an engagement with the number-one band in the nation.

So now I'm working at the Downbeat with Dizzy when one night this guy comes in. He says he's Benny Goodman's manager and they're over at the Earle Theater and Benny needs a drummer. Zoot Sims is in Benny's band and he's been coming to the Downbeat every night and Zoot, who's not much older than me, loves the way I play.

The King of Swing needs a drummer. The manager hears me and he likes me and he wants to introduce me to Benny. I say, "Sure, let's go!"

They take me backstage at the Earle. I've never been to any backstage in my life. The lights, the curtains, Benny Goodman. I'm gonna meet him! They take me to his dressing room, with a star on the door. Benny looks like a tailor, medium size. He has his back to me. I walk in, and . . . he's urinating in the sink! You see, the King don't walk to the bathroom! He turns around and he puts out his hand.

What do I do? I want the job—I gotta shake his hand.

I shook.

I go home and I'm all excited and I say, "Ma! I'm gonna be playing with Benny Goodman tomorrow morning, nine o'clock!" You see, he was so popular he could play these engagements of five shows every day for one or two weeks, and the first show started at nine o'clock in the morning.

She says, "Shut up and go to sleep."

She doesn't believe me. How could she believe me?

So I go in the next day and I play the first show. The lights come on, the curtain goes up. I'm sixteen years old, I've never played with a big band, I've never read music, I don't have my own drums and I've never even been on a real stage before. I was an unguided missile, but here I am playing with Benny Goodman, the number-one band in the country!

I fake it all the way through. What the heck am I doing up here? The lights, the Pearl drums. The Earle is one of those big palaces. Big facade, owned by one of the studios in Hollywood—they owned the movie theaters at that time. It's beautiful. Beautiful box office. Big marquee with the lights: "Earle Theater" in big bulbs. The foyer is beautifully carpeted. Open seating. Big stage, real big stage. Good lighting, theater lighting, very ornate, rococo, big balcony, big theater, fifteen hundred seats maybe, the balcony curved around. And they have a pit band, too, a sixteen-piece pit band that plays during the intermissions and during the newsreel. The pit band plays three or four numbers, then after ten minutes of that, Benny Goodman starts his theme and everybody says, "Hey Benny!" Then the curtain slowly opens and you start your show. Guaranteed sold out.

After that first show, I call up my mother again and I say, "Ma! Come down, I'm playing with Benny!"

"Will you stop?"

So, finally the second show goes on. And there in the front row is my mother, and her mouth is open three feet. "Benny Goodman! You? What!" Usually, every time I see her, my heart stops, I want to crawl inside the bass drum. But this one time, her mouth never shuts, and I keep looking at her. Benny turns to the band and introduces each of the players, except me. Then I hear my mother pipe up, "Hey Benny! Who's the drummer?"

Benny kept me on through the engagement but he never once looked at me. Not once did he announce my name to the audience. After we were introduced in his dressing room, he did not say one word to me. I found out later he didn't really like drummers.

Later he had a guy with him in New York by the name of Jumbo Brown—never to be heard from again—but they're playing in front of twelve or thirteen thousand people at the Paramount Theater. Benny goes into his trance. The drums are up on a riser, and he walked around and unscrewed the beater ball from the bass drum, takes it out, looks at it, and puts it in his pocket. That's the kind of stuff he did. Weird guy. He couldn't remember the names of his own family. He called everybody "Pops." He calls his kid: "Hey Pops, come over here." Calls his wife: "Come here, Pops!"

After the engagement, Benny's brother Irving issued train tickets to all the band members except me. He comes to me and says, "Benny says you should go home."

But at sixteen—even if only for a week—I played with the King.

Without more than a few scattered drum lessons, Stan was playing with the nation's most popular orchestra and its most innovative trumpet player. If he was hurt at being ignored by Goodman, Stan was buoyed by his growing relationship with Dizzy, who was a strong role model even beyond music.

"He was a master teacher," said Stan, "and he was voracious in his desire to succeed. He was a musician *and* a businessman."

Nickname notwithstanding, Dizzy was focused, responsible, and in a committed marriage. For a teenager like Stan who came from a fractured family, Dizzy Gillespie was someone he trusted and admired like an older brother.

Other young musicians—many of Philly's finest—came to the Downbeat to listen and sit in. As Dizzy's drummer, Stan either met or played with John Coltrane, Philly Joe Jones, the Heath Brothers, Buddy DeFranco, Red Rodney, and Herb Ellis. Playing with Goodman was a fleeting thrill, but Dizzy and the Downbeat offered security, a sense of family, and a social life. Stan was devastated when it ended.

Dizzy said he was moving to New York. That was it. The gig was finished. I felt terrible. I felt abandoned.

Then something new and terrible comes into my life. Nick Travis is a good trumpet player. He's kind of a hip, hangin' out kind of a guy. Basically a nice guy. We get to know each other. He's not too much older than me, but he comes with the best bands to the Earle Theater, and one time he says, "Man, I'm tired. You want some bennies?"

Who? I don't know what he's talking about—bennies. So he says, "Yeah, you put that in a Coke and you drink it." Okay. So I do that and I jump up and down for three days. So that's how it starts, and the next time he comes by he says, "Hey, we're gonna smoke some pot." And then we do that. I want to be part of that life. 'Cause I have no direction, no foundation, nothing. I'm hanging out there on a cliff. That's the start. I'm ripe for the drug scene. Ripe.

Family, school, and the Downbeat were all finished. The one thing Stan still had was boxing.

CHAPTER 2
THE FIGHT RACKET

Fight fans have long considered Philadelphia the number-one boxing town in the country, if not the world. Its reputation goes back to the nineteenth century, but the city became the undisputed boxing capital in 1926 when it turned out a staggering one hundred thousand spectators for the Jack Dempsey/Gene Tunney championship bout. Over the decades, Philly won bragging rights to over thirty world champions, including historic figures like Joe Frazier, Joey Giardello, and Tim Witherspoon. Nowhere else was the boxing business as much a part of city life as it was in the City of Brotherly Love. Philly was the natural setting for the movie *Rocky,* and the authenticity of the gritty Philly cityscapes helped make it one of the most beloved films in American cinema. For a tough young son of Philly like Stan Levey, entering boxing was a natural choice.

In Philly you had extreme competition. All the different gyms had rivalries. Every ethnic group had its own favorites, and I did pretty well as a white Jewish heavyweight.

My first fight, I'm nervous, very nervous. Italian guy—Forte—and he's a good boxer, good mover. I'm about seventeen. I'm ready. I train. Dick Kane is the trainer, he's had a stroke and only one side works. He drags that leg and the arm, and the head is way over, but he knows what the hell he's doing. He pushes me in the ring, training. When he trains you in the gym, he has a long yardstick. "You son of a bitch, get that left hand up!" *Whack!* He whacks you with that stick. He's good, a great trainer. He trains Bob Montgomery, Ike Williams—world champions. We never get into what he thinks about my father.

Day of the fight, I keep it quiet, I don't know if my mother knows or she doesn't know. I'm not communicating with her. Dave's not there.

You go in, take your clothes off, put on your athletic supporter and metal cup, get into your trunks, get taped, then the commissioner comes in and examines the wraps, then he puts his autograph on them. Then it's okay and you're ready, man. The gloves go on, you hit the rubbing table, and you rest. Then you got to warm up. Have to break a sweat.

Dick tells me, "Levey, you're up!" Walk out, robe on, towel around my neck, Vaseline on my face. Showtime.

You don't see the lights, any of that. You're in there to go to work. It's a hitting business. You give the hit, you take the hit. There's no mystique about it. You're focused on your opponent—that's it.

You're called to ring center. The referee says, "You know what to do, you've got your instructions. Keep your punches above the belt, no rabbit punching, no elbows, no stepping on the shoe." That's it. "Touch gloves. Let's go."

Not a whole lot of people on my side. But you don't pay any attention to it. You're there to do your work. Moving, cutting, boxing, and hitting. You never look for a knockout, you never look for that unless you see the guy get hurt; you hurt a guy and you try to do it.

He can hit, a good hitter. Doesn't put me down, hell no. I

beat him on a split decision. Four-round fight. Dick gives me a good pat on the back.

For the Mafioso, an association with the manliest of sports was practically essential. Huge money was wagered through mob-connected bookies, and the sport provided lucrative opportunities to manipulate odds and outcomes. To own a fighter, or even a piece of one, was a symbol of high status. Every wise guy in the nation wanted ringside seats and a cut of the action, but even as the various crime families jockeyed for influence and opportunities, everyone in the underworld understood that Frankie Carbo was the undisputed boss of boxing. Carbo's right-hand man was a close associate of Dave Levey's named Frank Palermo, a South Philly wise guy known coast to coast as "Blinky."

He shoplifted candy bars constantly, but Blinky Palermo was no small-time crook. He had the largest stable of fighters in the country and also controlled the Boxing Managers Guild. Palermo and Dave Levey traded fighters, shared sparring partners, took turns fronting for each other as silent partners, and conspired together to throw fights. Palermo was a regular visitor to an office Dave kept at 324 North Broad Street, and theirs was a relationship that typified the culture of the Boxing Managers Guild, a group that sports historian Steven A. Riess described as "mainly either upwardly mobile Jewish businessmen or Jewish and Italian hoodlums."

Carbo and Palermo pulled all the important strings in the business, determining who got choice bouts, controlling televised boxing, deciding where a fighter or manager could work, and choosing which venues got which fights. Under Carbo and Palermo's supervision, the mob was one of the facts of life in boxing. Trainer Angelo Dundee confirmed, "If you were

in boxing, somewhere along the line you had to do business
with them."

Everybody works through Frankie Carbo and Frankie Palermo. They control the whole thing. You don't work with
them? You don't work.

Around the gyms, they show up with the snap-brim hat,
the three-hundred-dollar overcoat. You know who they are.
You just don't talk to them. You don't approach them. They
see how the meat's doing here today, see how the guy looks,
cause they make the matches, they make the odds, they control everything.

Blinky's forty-three—something like that. A medi-
um-sized guy, five-seven, whatever. Slight build, pointed
features. Very dark eyes. Deep pools. Frankie Carbo is Mr.
Gray. Everyone calls him Mr. Gray. That's his name—don't
wear it out. These guys in those days are the worst.

This one fight, I'm the favorite. Palermo walks in with the
overcoat, and he slides his thumb behind the lapel and lays
three fingers down like that. Nothing. Not a word. And he
looks at me, waits to see a glimmer of understanding. I have
to go in the tank in the third, that's where the betting is, that
round. I'm ready to win. I know I can beat the guy. Nothing I
can do about it. You're resigned to what you're doing.

They run everything. You want to keep working? Do
what you're told and don't screw up. And when you do that,
you get an extra piece of money, too, cause they bet for
you, see. They're gonna lay out some money, you know, up
front they're gonna lay some money for you. So you get your
purse plus the bet. A business. Not that easy, cause when
you go in the tank—take a dive—the guy can't just graze
your head and you fall down and you wait ten. It don't go

that way, they'll yank your license and everything else. You gotta go in, you gotta take that shot, or several. It's gotta look right. And you get your head busted taking that shot, too. If you're going down in the third, at some point in the round you've gotta take that shot. It's just inches. Just drop your glove. Instead of where it's supposed to be, it's there.

I take two or three shots. I take two in the stomach and one up here, but I take them. And he hurts me. I can get up, but I just lay there. It looks good. I take what I have to take. I get paid for taking those three shots. About a week later, a runner comes over. They shake your hand: "Nice fight." And *boom*. You've got the money right there. Cash. The purse is set, you don't get more if you win or you lose. You sign, the money's there, and that's it.

Fighting and drumming are both all about hitting and timing. In those early years, I was boxing professionally as a heavyweight to earn a few extra dollars. I fought at Madison Square Garden and I was one of the preliminary bouts at the polo grounds in the Bronx when Joe Louis was the headliner. I carried on fighting until 1949. I boxed a lot of very good fighters . . . who beat the crap out of me! I could've made extra money wearing advertisements on the soles of my shoes.

American organized crime was also deep into jazz. Fellow travelers in the cultural landscape, the American Mafia and jazz music were both born in New Orleans and grew up together in Chicago, Kansas City, and New York.

Pianist Mary Lou Williams, who helped develop the Kansas City Sound and was know as the "First Lady of Jazz" remembered the K.C. scene: "Most of the jazz spots were run by politicians and hoodlums, and the town was wide open for drinking, gambling, and pretty much every form of vice. . . .

Kansas City boasted everything New York had."

That included the Mafia. The Kansas City Outfit, bound by the same pinprick to the finger and blood oath that bonded all the families, controlled the police department and operated overtly—as much a part of city life as potholes and parking meters. In the population frequenting their clubs, the gangsters saw a market for something only their well-connected network could provide: pure heroin from overseas. The K.C. family ran what was thought to be the largest ring in the country in the 1930s. They worked with native Sicilians and the Tampa family to import French Connection powder and spread it all over the Midwest. They brought it into their clubs (where musicians could be counted on as reliable consumers of intoxicants), and dumped it in the black neighborhoods, where an aspiring saxophonist named Charlie Parker was only fifteen years old when he got hooked on Mafia heroin and began pawning his mother's appliances to get his fix.

Parker lived near Eighteenth and Vine Streets, where musicians flocked for late-night jam sessions and highly competitive "cutting contests." Count Basie, Lester Young, Hot Lips Page, Ben Webster, Jo Jones, Jay McShann, Big Joe Turner, and other heavyweight talents traded punches in the form of fierce and emotional improvisations. Bassist Gene Ramey offered his take on the scene: "Jam sessions in a sense were constant trials of manhood. Different sections of the band would set difficult riffs behind soloists, and, sometimes, they would see if they could lose each other."

It was at one such jam session that young Charlie Parker summoned the courage to sit in and blow. Drummer Jo Jones, acting on behalf of all the cats, abruptly ended Parker's participation by throwing a cymbal at the teenage saxophonist. In jazz lore, it is one of the great story arcs in the history of the music—a humiliation that would later be avenged beyond anyone's musical imagination.

"This gave Bird a big determination to play," remembered Gene Ramey. "'I'll fix these cats,' he used to say. 'Everybody's laughing at me now, but just wait and see.'"

When the time came, Stan Levey would be in Charlie Parker's corner.

CHAPTER 3

FIFTY-SECOND STREET

I'm about seventeen, still working for my old man in the daytime selling cars, fighting when I get a chance. Before he left, Dizzy and also a very light-skinned black guy named Carl Warwick, great guy—we called him "Bama"—they told me I should come to New York, that they'd help me once I got there. I'm really ready to go.

I'm a pretty strong kid. I always looked older than I was. I'm big. I'm walking down Market Street, which is the main drag where the Earle Theater is. Then I turn onto Eleventh and I'm just strolling into midtown, and as I'm walking by, there's a guy. I don't see the guy, but I hear, "Hey, get over here!"

I just hear it, I don't know what he's talking about. "Hey, get over here!" Like that, so I turn my head to see what's going on. "Who? What?" And he says, "You!" This guy—big guy, a *starker*—standing in a doorway with a hat on, a snap-brimmed hat, and I look at him real close and he says, "Yeah you, come here."

So I don't move. I freeze. I'm thinking, "What the hell is this?" So he comes over to me and I'm still standing near the curb. I haven't answered him. I don't know who he is.

He says, "Get over here, now." I see the look in his eye. I'm starting to get worried.

He grabs me. He puts his arm around my neck and somehow gets my left arm bent up in my back, that kind of a hold, and he's struggling with me, and I say, "What the . . . " I can't believe what's happening to me. Can't believe it. I yell, "Who are you? What are you doing?" I can't believe this guy. He says, "Shut up!" Everything races through my mind. Am I being held up in broad daylight? People are looking, people are stopped and looking. I'm saying, "Get off of me, you son of a bitch!" He says, "Shut up!" He doesn't identify himself. Nothing, nothing, zero.

We're struggling and struggling. I'm a strong kid, and we work each other down to the ground. As we hit the pavement, we're half on the curb, half on the street, and he's got a chokehold around my neck. I'm thinking, "I'm gonna die, I can't get any air. I'm being murdered. This guy is crazy." I have my right arm free, but I can't breathe, I feel his body right up behind, so I take my right arm back and I hit him a shot in the ribs, God, I really give him a shot. With that, his hands release on my neck.

In my mind, at that second, I know I've got to kill him 'cause I've got a man that's trying to kill me. I turn around. I'm very quick, and he's on the bottom, with his legs on the street, body on the curb. I'm looking at him. Do I know him? I work my way up to my knees and he's still hurting pretty good but he's still got a hold of me. He's got me by my collar and I can't get away, and I see that he's lying halfway down. His knee is on the curb and it's half on the street, and see, there's only one thing I can do. My legs are free and I bolt upright and I slam my foot down on his leg and I hear a crack. I break his leg, man.

I get up and I'm trying to get my breath, can't believe what is happening. Now I'm getting out of here, I don't want to know who he is. He says, "Stop! Police!" And he's hurting. He goes inside his coat, he's fumbling, and he pulls out a badge. He says, "Stop or I'll shoot!" Now everybody hears it, everybody splits and I start running down Eleventh, and he shoots. Creased me right here on the ankle. He could've killed somebody. I'm bleeding pretty good. In those days, that's what they do. Could've killed me if he hit me right. He never identifies himself. I must look like somebody in a poster. God knows, that's all it could be. I don't know him, he don't know me. If he says, "I'm a policeman, let's go downtown," fine, let's go downtown, there's no problem. But they don't do that. They do whatever they want in 1943.

That shakes me up. It was the worst thing that had happened to me in my life, up to that point. I know I'm in trouble. He doesn't know who I am, but I'm scared to walk downtown. They all have a description, they're looking for that description. Regardless of whether I did anything before, now I did something.

I'd been planning to leave anyway and this is a definite exit number. My friend, Ellis Tollin, we've been talking about it. He wants to go to New York. I say, "Fine, let's go."

When I tell my mother I'm going to New York, she does a fake, "Ohhh, you can't go, that's a terrible city. You can't go."

"I'm leaving Thursday, and you'll hear from me." And I just go. And I know she does a sigh of relief once I leave.

Ellis is ready. Good buddy. He has a nice drum set. His father drives us to New York and we take a top-floor room in the Schuyler Hotel on Forty-Sixth. First thing I do is hit "The Street."

Fifty-Second Street evolved from a row of gangster speak-easies into the jazz capital of the world in the 1940s. Clubs lined both sides of the street between Fifth and Seventh Avenues. None were particularly plush. Most were bare-bones basements equipped with cramped bandstands and tiny tables, but on any given night, the bright marquees were lit with the biggest names in jazz, all within less than two blocks. Fifty-Second Street represented the pinnacle of the jazz district, the culmination of Storyville in New Orleans and Eighteenth and Vine in Kansas City. For Stan Levey and other teenage arrivals like Quincy Jones, it was a cup of overflowing excitement.

Inside every doorway was one of my heroes. It was pulsating and alive. Electric. That period in the 1940s, the years when bebop was surfacing, creativity and the excitement that goes along with it were at a really high level. The music was just as pure as it could be.

"We were some of the luckiest people alive," Quincy Jones said, "because we got a chance to not only participate in some of the best music that was ever made, but also to *hear* some of the best music ever made—the Birds, the Lesters, Basie and Ella and Sarah. Duke and Dizzy, Miles . . . I wouldn't trade this time when Stan and I came up for any other time."

So Dizzy introduces me to Specs Powell. Says to Specs, "This guy can play!" Specs is drumming for Ben Webster, but he has another gig, so he arranges for me to audition for Ben. I go into the Three Deuces and Ben is big and mean-looking. Intimidating. I try to play Spec's drums but he tunes them too soft for me. I don't play well. Everything was soggy and Ben doesn't like it and he doesn't hire me. My first audition in New York—a disaster. Now my confidence is real low.

But then Diz introduces me to Oscar Pettiford, who needs a drummer. Diz says to Oscar—and this is the kind of guy Dizzy is—he says, "Here's your new drummer."

So Oscar hires me on the spot for a week-long engagement at the Tick Tock Club in Boston. So I steal Ellis's drums and off we go to Boston, where we play a lot of Dizzy's music, which I already know how to play. It was a hell of a band, with Flip Tate on trumpet. The tenor man was Johnny Hosfield. Oscar liked to drink and, being an Indian, he could get pretty rough. But with me he was always just a great, beautiful guy.

I learn a lot and they really like me. At the end of that gig at the Tick Tock, who comes in? Billy Eckstine's band with Dexter Gordon, Miles Davis, Art Blakey, Gene Ammons, Sarah Vaughan . . . they were the hippest band playing this very heavy music. Art Blakey was beginning to get into a modern groove. Technique-wise, he was a diamond in the rough, but he had that hard swing that could swing you right off the bandstand. I was on top of the world.

It was a grand gesture on the part of Dizzy Gillespie. Oscar Pettiford was the most highly regarded bassist on the scene. By vouching for the teenage drummer, Dizzy was staking his reputation with the A-list of American musicians. It bespoke a confidence in Stan that the drummer never forgot. For the rest of his life, Stan would give credit to Dizzy Gillespie as his most influential figure and his greatest teacher.

After returning to New York from Boston, Stan landed a gig subbing for Denzil Best in Coleman Hawkins's band, a sextet that included trumpeter Benny Harris and Thelonious Monk on piano.

The bass player—nobody knows about this guy—was one of the best I've ever heard. His name was Eddie Robinson, and they called him "Bassie." He got into trouble . . . I think it was guns and drugs. But that guy could really play.

I learned so much listening to Monk and Hawkins. People thought Monk was crazy, but part of that was a façade. Monk looked totally unaware, like a space cadet, but he was aware of everything. Hawkins was like a prince, with his perfect clothing. The younger musicians were in awe of him. His ears were always open to new music, and he always urged you on to play better. He was very competitive. He'd show up at a jam session and say, "I was just walking by and happened to have my horn."

Thelonious Monk and Coleman Hawkins were formidable influences, but it was Max Roach that Stan studied for ideas and inspiration on the skins. The most iconic of the bebop drummers, Roach was two years older than Stan, and was creating a sensation with Dizzy and Pettiford at the Onyx Club. Roach would have countless disciples over the next fifty years, but Stan was his first "student" and his most ardent fan.

When I heard Max, it was like lightning had struck. I almost passed out. I went crazy. I got as close to the bandstand as I could; I had to get a better idea of what he was up to. The ferocity of the playing was new to me. I had never heard time split up like that.

Max's playing had music within it. Whenever I could, I got up very close to him in a club and observed. Max was breaking things up between his hands and feet in a manner that, at first, was puzzling. Those techniques had not been used in just that way before. When you finally caught on to what he was all about, it was a revelation. He changed the course of drumming. Because of him, a drummer had to offer something extra—color the music, and give it a more well-rounded feeling.

Max was responsible for developing my concept of music. He had an underlying intensity and spirit, particularly on the up-tempo things, that I tried to capture in my own work. Now, I emulated him, but I didn't copy him. We shared an apartment for a while and became very close friends. I got to know his mother well.

Stan would remain fiercely loyal to Max for the rest of his life and would tolerate no denigration of Roach's playing. The two young drummers spent the rest of the 1940s trading jobs in the hippest bands on Fifty-Second Street, but unlike Max, who studied the instrument formally, Stan relied on his natural aptitude and ability to absorb ideas quickly.

"He was like a sponge," said Stan's wife, Angela. "Later, when we moved to California, he had never associated with neighbors before. He had never engaged in that type of social life. He just watched me and before long he was everybody's favorite."

Stan's self-taught style epitomized the "feel" associated with jazz. His innate rhythm gave rise to a natural sound that seemed effortless and free. He played fast tempos with a fluidity that allowed soloists to fly on steady currents of unwavering time, uncluttered by bombast or affectation, yet strong with the potent accents of modern jazz. Dizzy Gillespie said of Stan, "He had the most feeling of any of those white drummers who picked up on modern jazz early, guys like Shelly Manne, Irv Kluger, and Dave Tough."

I turned away from certain kinds of drummers—the bangers. They were machinery, hardware. I wasn't interested in players whose pulse didn't flow. There had to be a sense of motion. I didn't want to plod through four beats of each bar just to get to the end of the tune. I wanted everything to swing. When musicians looked back and smiled, I knew I was doing it.

I'm a big one for simplicity. Unfortunately, a lot of drummers go into overkill when there's a short solo to be played or a space to be filled in a chart. I believe in keeping things pretty straightforward. You tend to be more efficient that way. There's no need to throw a whole career into a break. It's really very distracting. It slows the momentum of the band and doesn't enhance the swing in any way.

Stan's first steady job on The Street was with Barney Bigard, who made a name for himself as Duke Ellington's clarinetist. One night in 1944, Stan was working the Onyx Club with Bigard when Sugar Ray Robinson, future middleweight champion of the world, came in and asked Stan if he could sit in on drums.

He's not great, but the hands work and he does pretty good. We talk about some of the people we know. We don't mention Palermo or Frankie Carbo or anybody like that. You don't talk about them.

Years later, Stan and Hoagy Carmichael Jr. went to the Los Angeles Sports Arena to see Sugar Ray fight Gene Fulmer for the NBA middleweight title. "Robinson was near the end of his career," said Carmichael, "and they called it a draw: a decision that both Stan and I felt was predetermined."

Then I get a call from Leonard Feather, the well-known English critic and record producer. He recognized me as an up-and-comer and called me to do a record date for the Black and White label.

Wow! My first record date! Just tell me where and when! I borrowed Ellis's drums and went into the Reman Scott Studios on Fifty-Second Street, near Sixth Avenue. I went up there, got off the elevator, went into the studio, and stopped cold in my tracks.

There at the piano . . . sitting there playing . . . was Art Tatum.

A more musically intimidating figure did not exist. Described as "superhuman" by his peers, the blind pianist played like a man possessed, transforming a keyboard into a full orchestra with his ambidextrous hands and supersonic ears. Tatum could tell the type of coin dropped on a table by the sound it made.

With his head-spinning technique and avalanche of improvisational ideas, Tatum's early recordings made young pianists like Hank Jones and Oscar Peterson think two or even three people were playing. Even to this day, Tatum remains in a class by himself, separate from the continuum of jazz pianists whose innovations were absorbed by younger generations. "First you speak of Art Tatum," explained Dizzy Gillespie, "then take a long, deep breath . . . and then you speak of the other pianists."

I did a one-eighty and started walking out. Leonard Feather said, "Where are you going?" I said, "I cannot play with Art Tatum. I wouldn't even think of it. He's way above my ability." He says, "Get back in there. You can do it."

> I went back in and I set up. It was kind of a mish-mash
> of a band, Georgie Auld, Joe Thomas, the guitar player was
> Chuck Wayne. I played very softly and tried to just fit in. Art
> came over—he was blind—and he put his arm around me.
> He said, "You did real, real good." Boy did that help me in
> this career that I had . . . I'll never forget him for that.

Stan's next gig was with the most exciting pianist since
Art Tatum himself. Erroll Garner couldn't read music and
had to sit on a telephone book to reach the keys, but his en-
chanting and highly individualistic playing made him one of
the top-selling jazz artists ever. Fresh from Pittsburgh, Garner
mesmerized many a musician in his first performances on The
Street—including Stan, who approached Garner after a set
and landed a job with him that same night.

Between his work with Dizzy Gillespie, Oscar Pettiford,
Art Tatum, and Erroll Garner, the self-taught kid from Philly
was quickly establishing a quality résumé. Work became plenti-
ful, with Stan drumming for a variety of ensembles, including
the George Shearing Trio. After his stint with Shearing, Stan
joined Henry Jerome's band, notable for its oddball but auspicious personnel.

"It was by far the best band I ever played in," remembered
tenor saxophonist Alan Greenspan. "A surprising number of
my fellow musicians and our successors went on to memora-
ble careers. Johnny Mandel, one of our trombonists, went to
Hollywood and wrote 'The Shadow of Your Smile' and the
theme music for *M*A*S*H* and won an Academy Award and
four Grammys . . . Stan Levey later played with Charlie Parker.
Larry Rivers became a major pop artist. And my fellow sax
player, Lenny Garment, became President Nixon's lawyer."

In his book *Crazy Rhythm,* Garment took credit for

bringing Stan Levey to New York after meeting him at a jam session at the Downbeat Club in Philly. Stan remembered Garment as a very good tenor player and Larry Rivers as "completely crazy . . . he was cuckoo then, and he's nuts now. The guy's wacko, but a great artist." Alan Greenspan, of course, went on to become chairman of the Federal Reserve, and was widely labeled as one of the most powerful men in the world during his tenure. Not surprisingly, he doubled as the band's treasurer and paymaster.

Stan was also doing double duty. When the opportunity arose, he would take a fight at Sunnyside Gardens in Queens or back home in Philadelphia. Like many other journeyman fighters of the preliminary ranks, Stan sometimes fought under different names—such as the alias Joe Levy, with a record of three wins and four losses in fights held in New Jersey, Brooklyn, Hartford, and at the Valley Arena in Holyoke, Massachusetts. For boxers who threw the occasional fight, pseudonyms helped avoid the scrutiny of regulators. For Stan, they also served to keep his two careers separate from each other.

I'm doing both the fighting and the music but I never let one know what I do on the other end of it, because the musicians say, "Hey, this guy's a fighter," and I don't want that. I'm a drummer. And the boxers will say, "Hey, a musician—put your dress on!" To the musicians, this guy's scary. He's a fighter. They don't want to have him in the band. "Might get strange. Who knows, if he gets mad he might dump someone."

I have to eliminate that, which I do. Not their business, it's my business. It's how I make some money. I think Dizzy knows. I'm not a full-time fighter. They get me a match, the money's kinda right. I'd have a couple of weeks to get in shape and do the best I can.

On October 18, 1944, opening for a main event featuring his hometown hero, Ike Williams, Stan fought under the name "Sam Levey" in front of six thousand people at Memorial Auditorium in Buffalo, New York. Stan and Ike were both victorious, with Williams knocking out Johnny Green and Stan dropping Ben Tyler in the second round of a four-round fight.

CHAPTER 4

THE BIRD FLIES IN

All this time I'm on Fifty-Second Street, working up and down, I'd hear people saying, "The Bird is coming!" The Bird is coming? What bird? A sparrow? A robin? A pigeon?

Charlie Parker.

After his hometown humiliation in Kansas City, Charlie Parker took a summer job in the Ozarks, where he "went to the woodshed," practicing his horn in stretches of up to twelve solitary hours, concentrating and learning to play tunes in *every* key.

Parker returned to K.C. a transformed musician and landed a job playing swing and jump blues with pianist and bandleader Jay "Hootie" McShann. McShann shared how Parker got his nickname:

"We were in two cars, and the car he was in drove over a chicken, and Bird put his hands on his head and said, 'No, stop! Go back and pick up that yardbird!' He insisted on it and we went back and Bird got out of the car and carefully wrapped up the chicken and took it with him to the hotel where we were staying and made the cook there cook it for us. He told him we had to have this yardbird. Whenever he saw some chicken on the menu, he'd say, 'Give me some of the yardbird over there.'"

As Parker soared ever higher on his saxophone, "Yard-bird" was shortened to "Bird." Dizzy Gillespie and a few other friends called him "Yard."

In his role as star saxophonist for Jay McShann, Parker was a key participant in one of the most legendary of the big band battles. The Savoy Ballroom showdown between Jay McShann and Lucky Millinder became the most celebrated battle since Chick Webb lost his life to tuberculosis of the spine in 1939. From Webb, Millinder inherited the house band position at the Savoy, and with it, the status of *the* band to beat for aspiring challengers.

Millinder's boys, resplendent in their sharp uniforms, laughed at the cheap suits and cardboard stands of the McShanns, who rolled into New York at the last minute, sweaty, hungry, and rumpled after an epic road trip from Kansas City. Just before the contest, the Millinders sent the McShanns a note that said, "We're going to send you hicks back to the sticks!"

It was his big chance, and McShann employed classic boxing strategy.

"Lucky had been blowing everybody out of there, so he was supposed to be the baddest thing around New York," McShann remembered. "We decided to go in and lay low . . . play a few [stock arrangements] and fool around until the date was three-fourths over. . . . Every once in a while, old Bird would say, 'Hootie, you better get in the books, baby!' The next set, we got down in the books, so Lucky is raring to take his stand. He ran out there and started to do a lot of show stuff. He had the audience worked up . . . doing the Lindy Hop. Heavy stuff, but Lucky wasn't swinging. When he started with all of his show stuff, the band lost its beat. Soon as he finished his last note, we hit right in on him. Pulled the crowd completely away from Lucky. This was a thirty-minute number, and the people screamed and hollered for *another* thirty minutes.

"What really helped was having Bird in that big band. When Bird was in the section, you would see him turn, especially on those head tunes, he would be giving this cat his note. He'd give him the note he wanted him to make. He might tell 'em, and if he didn't tell 'em, he'd play it for 'em. And if you see him turning this way, he'd be giving this cat his note. Sometimes they'd get off on the wrong notes. Then after a while they would all come together."

McShann's bassist, Gene Ramey, later recalled, "When I look back, it seems to me that Bird was at the time so advanced in jazz that I do not think we realized to what degree his ideas had become perfected."

The McShann band recorded for Decca in 1940 and had a big hit with "Confessin' the Blues." Embedded like a secret treasure on the B-side of the record was a Parker solo on "Hootie Blues" that flew over the heads of most listeners but elicited a fascinated "Who the hell is *that?*" from musicians all over the country.

"He had a completely different approach in everything," said McShann. "Everything was completely different, just like when you change the furniture in the house and you come in and you won't know your own house."

Between intervals with McShann, Parker spent a little time washing dishes in New York. In a Harlem chili house in 1940, Parker had a musical epiphany widely acknowledged as a wellspring for bebop.

"Now, I'd been getting bored with the stereotyped changes that were being used all the time at the time," Parker said, "and I kept thinking there's bound to be something else. I could hear it sometimes, but I couldn't play it. Well, that night, I was working over 'Cherokee,' and as I did, I found that by using the higher intervals of a chord as a melody line and backing them with appropriately related changes, I could play the thing I'd been hearing. I came alive."

Back in Kansas City a few months later, "two halves of a musical heartbeat" came together for the first time near Eighteenth and Vine at Musicians Union Local 627. Charlie Parker and Dizzy Gillespie, in town with Cab Calloway's band, met and played together for the first time.

"I was astounded by what the guy could do," Dizzy recalled. "These other guys that I had been playing with weren't my colleagues, really. But the moment I heard Charlie Parker, I said, 'There is my colleague.' I had never heard anything like that before. The way that he assembled notes together. That was one of the greatest thrills . . . Charlie Parker and I were moving in practically the same direction."

The two got a chance to work together in 1943, in the Earl Hines Band. Hines hired Gillespie after Cab Calloway fired Dizzy, following an incident that illustrates the rough and tumble nature of the jazz music business at that time.

One of the highest compliments in jazz was, "He don't take shit off *nobody!*" The expression was a snarl at Jim Crow, referring to a black man who maintained his dignity even under oppression, but it extended into the day-to-day life of a hard-working road musician. History remembers Gillespie as a big sweetheart, but he had a tough and combative side, especially in his hungry years. He once snatched the eyeglasses right off the face of a bandleader who held out pay. When that didn't work, Dizzy dropped the bandleader onto the sidewalk with one solid punch.

Dizzy got into it with Calloway after the authoritarian bandleader blamed Dizzy for throwing a spitball on stage. Cab and Diz squared off in a hallway backstage. Calloway was a gifted athlete who could turn flips while singing. Quick as a rimshot, he landed a punch to Gillespie's face. Dizzy drew a knife and, amidst the chaos, cut Cab in leg, staining his razor-sharp, white custom stage suit with blood.

News of the incident spread quickly, but Earl Hines hired Gillespie anyway. No stranger to hot blood, Hines had just ended his long contract as the orchestra leader at Al Capone's Grand Terrace Ballroom in Chicago. "If they were going to run some beer from Detroit to Chicago, they'd figure the job out right in the kitchen," said Hines of the Chicago Outfit. "Our relations were always cordial, and sometimes it paid to know these fellows."

Hines was eager to hit the road and hire sharp young cats for his new band. After hiring Gillespie, he landed Charlie Parker, whom Jay McShann had reluctantly let go of due to Parker's increasing drug abuse and erratic behavior.

Offstage from the Hines band, the two modernists played together constantly and developed their fiery new form of musical expression, soon to be known as bebop. The orchestra soon became too limiting for the two pioneers. After brief stints with Billy Eckstine, both Dizzy and Bird headed for the small group scene on Fifty-Second Street.

I was working on Fifty-Second Street with different people—Barney Bigard, Coleman Hawkins. And this guy walks into the Downbeat Club. Monday night, open sessions. He looked like a used pork chop. Like he just rolled off a garbage truck. Shoes that don't match, pants with no belt. Shirt looks like he's slept in it for a month. His hair is standing straight up—looked like Don King. He's got his horn in a paper bag with rubber bands and cellophane on it and there he is, Charlie Parker.

"Well," I say, "this guy looks terrible. Can he play?"

Bird unwraps the horn from the paper bag and he gets up to play. And you never heard anything like it. Like the Pied Piper of Hamelin. Like he's talking to my brain in words. In sentences! I'm hearing what he's saying to me, he's speaking to me. It makes musical sense—punctuation, exclamation marks! I can't believe it. Nobody ever heard anything like it.

Seventeen years old and I have to play with this guy, I've been waiting all my life to play with this guy I've never heard till tonight, okay? When I get my chance, Parker doesn't acknowledge me. Just says, "Play the blues" to the piano player—Hank Jones, I think, or maybe Monk. We get into something real cooking, and he plays about eight bars and he looks back at me. I say, "Oh, he doesn't like me." And then he opens his mouth with that gold-rimmed tooth and that big grin, and from that moment on, we were like *this*. Musically bonded. It was the weirdest experience I ever had. An out-of-body experience. I would have followed him anywhere. Over the cliff, wherever.

Later that night, he says, "Man, you come home with me. You eat yourself something sweet, like a sweet roll."

"Huh?"

The two were an unlikely pair only on the surface. To Bird, who listened to Salvation Army bands with the same attentive curiosity he paid to Stravinsky, the self-taught white kid playing backwards was a natural choice. There were many more mature and polished drummers working New York, but in Stan Levey, Bird found the intense and quirky fire that was essential to bebop. It wasn't long before the Pied Piper asked Stan to join his band and share an apartment with him.

> So we go to an all-night place and eat a sweet roll, and he says, "We're going uptown now." I'm thinking, "Good, we're going to go play some more."
>
> But we don't play. We go up to his room at the Marionette Hotel. Colored hotel. A walk-up. Bird's got a room without a window, like a broom closet. Somebody shoehorned a bed in there. Filthy. Then he pulls out the needle, with a spoon and the powder, takes his tie, and he lifts it over his head and ties up his arm and he's cooking up, saying nothing. Taps the vein, hits it, blood comes up in the thing, then he starts squeezing. "Oh man, this is good . . . " Then when he gets through, he says, "You're next."
>
> I'm a kid. I don't even really know what this is, and I just say, "All right." And he cleans the needle and hits me, does the whole thing. No sooner does he get it in than I run down the hall to the common bathroom and throw up. That's why the sweet roll, cause it's sweet when it comes up.
>
> Nice story?

In the space of one night, Stan Levey experienced the steepest arc of his young life. Two life-changing events, both orchestrated by Bird, rocked his world in the space of a few hours. He'd become blood brothers with the most innovative, but also the most volatile, musician of his generation, and there was no turning back. According to Stan, from that point on, his life as roommate to Charlie Parker was "like living in the eye of a hurricane."

The musical bond between Stan and Bird was real, but there was another reason Bird gravitated towards big Stan: he needed somebody to help him get his fix.

From that day on, I was hooked. The chase was on. Like a dog chasing its tail. They smuggled it in ships. Freighters. These guys would package the heroin in oil-tight packaging and slip it into these big oil pans underneath the engines. That's how they got it over here.

The reason Bird turns people on is to get them involved. Once you're in the club . . . then we all go out and hustle money. He gets some of my dope. When he's low, he's got a friend to go to. When a pusher gets tough, or some junkie gets dangerous, he's got me to protect him. He'll say, "Give me ten dollars and I'll score." He scores—takes half the stuff—shorts me. He wouldn't shoot up with just anyone. [To] lots of guys, he wouldn't ever admit he used.

But Bird alone did not bear full responsibility for corrupting the teenager with the evil injection. The needle the two musicians shared in that windowless apartment in Harlem was symbolically stained with the blood of pinprick ceremonies held in the Italian part of Kansas City.

Without even realizing it, Stan was taking another dive for the mob.

CHAPTER 5

BEBOP

Bird's arrival completed the assembly of bebop pioneers in New York. Stan was the youngest member of this small group of history-making musicians led by Gillespie and Parker, who, in Dizzy's words, became "two halves of the same heartbeat."

"There was never anybody who played any closer than we did," Gillespie reminisced. "Sometimes, I couldn't tell whether I was playing or not because the notes were so close together . . . "

[Dizzy and Bird] played very, very fast. They had great technique, great ideas. They ran their lines through the chord changes differently than anyone else. Prior to them, it was Roy Eldridge, Coleman Hawkins, that type of thing. This was a complete left-hand turn with the music. It was wonderful. When I heard this thing, I said it was for me. I got connected.

Leonard Feather, the on-the-scene scribe of early bebop, stated that the "first genuine all-bebop group" was Dizzy's band with Charlie Parker, Stan, pianist Al Haig, and bassist Curly Russell.

"I remember seeing Stan Levey's name up there with

Bird," Quincy Jones said. "That was that first team, man."

As one of the few true bebop pioneers, Stan had a form of street cred that was rare in the music business. His history as a bebop pioneer would set him apart from his peers for the rest of his career.

Bebop was characterized by breakneck tempos, disorienting rhythms, hip chord substitutions, and dissonant tritones—also called "flatted fifths," which gave the music its characteristically unresolved phrase endings. It was drenched with modernism in the form of what jazz historian Martin Williams called "melodic rhythm." Boppers rewrote the rules, playing "wrong" notes and risky accents. Vibrato was minimized, and notes—*flurries* of them—were emphasized. Like boxing, bebop was a test of a man's endurance. "It took extraordinary mental and physical discipline," said jazz critic Kevin Whitehead. "Boppers had to think fast to play fast."

> Not many dug what we were trying to do; most came by the Deuces, the Onyx, or the Spotlite because they had heard there was some really weird new music being played. It was like a freak show, I guess, and the musicians were the freaks.

The intensity of bebop became a metaphor for the quickening of postwar life in a more urban and industrial, but still segregated, United States. Bebop was black music that expressed frustration, anger, and sarcastic humor. With nary one lyric, the music captured perfectly the sound of a growing impatience. Men who had risked their lives in the Second World War were no longer content to wait for their own country to treat them equally.

Bebop presented the American black man as intellectual virtuoso, proud and non-subservient—concerned with art, not entertainment. Ralph Ellison wrote, "Bop sprang partially from their desire to create a jazz which could not be so easily imitated and exploited by white musicians to whom the market was more open simply *because* of their whiteness."

The blackness of bebop is extensively documented and well-understood, but the interracial aspects of bop, as personified by Stan Levey, are also vital to the music's history.

The African American musicians who molded bop out of the Negro experience were in the business of breaking down barriers. One of the most direct ways to challenge segregation was to have a mixed band. Jazz was always the fiercest of meritocracies, and certainly no black bandleader ever hired a sub-par white cat just to make a political statement. But at the dawn of bebop, the sight of a white musician in a black band was exceedingly rare. By rejecting the orthodoxy that a black man's authority to hire and fire whomever he pleased was limited to other blacks, Gillespie asserted himself as an independent participant in the free market. The history of the music is littered with ugly anecdotes of black (and white) musicians being exploited by record companies and concert promoters. "Taking shit off nobody" meant being a tough and savvy negotiator. Gillespie and many other jazz artists became ambitious entrepreneurs and, eventually, wealthy businessmen. Stan was proud of his friend's thrift, business acumen, and financial success. "Look at him today," Stan boasted shortly before Dizzy's death. "Worth a hundred million dollars."

Stan's presence on the bandstand challenged other conventions as well, including the notion that bop was designed to keep whites out. Levey proved that whites could play bebop before anyone got around to suggesting they couldn't. With the alluring Al Haig on piano, "the first genuine all-bebop band," as Leonard Feather called it, was two-fifths white. The mixed band was a reflection of the non-racist and pro-merit attitudes of Dizzy and Bird.

"Black drummers would come up to Dizzy and say, 'Hey man, how come you got that white boy playing?'" Stan recalled. "And Dizzy would just straight ahead say, 'Hey, when you can play better than him—not as good, but better—you'll have the job.'" Of Bird, trumpeter Benny Harris said, "He had just as many white friends as colored. He liked company."

Still, bop was a thoroughly Negro art form and Stan's experience was unusual, especially since his participation extended from the bandstand into the Harlem apartments and personal lives of his African American friends and roommates.

So Bird and I got a bigger place and started rooming together in Harlem, between Broadway and Amsterdam. Rooming house. One bed. We shared it. Sometimes in shifts, sometimes together.

He'd wake up in middle of the night writing tunes. Just start playing his horn. One night he woke up at 3:00 AM, jumped out of bed, and wrote "Confirmation." He was very literate. Conversed intelligently on many subjects. A voracious reader. This is a guy that used to play chess with Russians, but he was also one of the greatest con men that ever lived. He'd con your pants off. Bird was a paranoid schizophrenic—a sociopath. I want—I take. That's it. I had to hide my wallet. Sometimes he doesn't show up for three or four days at a time. He was always on the mooch and he was a voracious eater. Eat three dinners at a time. He never had any real money. "Give me the advance," you know. Get in the cab and go. He was an unguided missile. Minute-to-minute, not even day-to-day. You couldn't nail him down. You took him as he was. You didn't try to change him. He was like quicksilver.

The mercurial details of the first Bird–led band have proven elusive.

"There were so many things taking place then," said Parker of his early efforts in New York. "It's hard to describe it because it all happened in a matter of months."

Chuck Haddix, author of *Bird: The Life and Music of Charlie Parker*, wrote that Bird's first band consisted of Don Byas on tenor, Al Haig on piano, Curly Russell on bass, and Stan on drums. Stan said that Parker's first band was a bass-less trio of Bird, himself, and Hank Jones on piano with Joe Albany substituting. The only thing that appears certain about Bird's first band was that Stan was in it, but much of Stan's playing with Bird during this time took place not within a formalized ensemble but in the myriad jam sessions of Harlem.

We used to play all night on Fifty-Second Street. And then we'd go up to Minton's and jam. Why the super fast tempos? To show that playing them was possible, and sometimes to drive people away. At Minton's there was this saxophone player called "Horse Collar." He couldn't play anything. To discourage him and others—to keep them off the stand—the guys would go into a fantastically brisk tempo and wipe them out. It was a way of saying, "If you can't do this, don't even think about coming around to play with us."

We all knew who the pushers were, and we'd see them walking by the clubs. We wanted to catch them before they moved on, so we'd play the "Fifty-Second Street Theme" at the end of the set, so damn fast it was amazing. I don't know how we did it. *Doodoo-dah-bebop!* Stop, sticks down, out the door. I had no difficulty with Bird's tempos. Don't ask me how, but I was able to play as fast as anybody wanted. I could play "up" pretty easily. I could play very, very fast. It was a gift. I had nothing to do with it.

If anyone played more jam sessions with Bird than me, I don't know who that would be.

As Bird and Stan jammed around Manhattan, they came into contact with many of the older cats from Kansas City. Ben Webster, Lips Page, Lester Young, and others were headlining Fifty-Second Street after migrating from K.C. How well these players remembered the boy who got "gonged off" by Joe Jones is unclear, but one thing was for sure: nobody was laughing now.

Back at Eighteenth and Vine, Bird had bugged them by constantly hanging around and bumming cigarettes. Now he was testing everything they knew and understood about the craft they'd spent their lives mastering. One account has a bewildered Ben Webster, upon first hearing Bird in New York, grabbing Bird's saxophone away and exclaiming, "That horn ain't supposed to sound that fast!"

When young Charlie Parker said to Gene Ramey, "I'll fix these cats," there can be little doubt that in Parker's mind, Ben Webster was one of the cats who needed fixing. Born within walking distance of Bird's adolescent home, Webster was one of the most competitive men to come out of the K.C. jam sessions, and one of the most original and individual voices ever to play the tenor saxophone.

Stan sympathized with Parker. Having been rejected by Webster at his first audition in New York, the newly confident drummer also had something to prove. Bird and Stan got their chance when Webster hired them.

He heard that we were the latest thing, so he wanted to have us in the band, which he did. He hired us. The first night went pretty well and the second night . . . Ben likes to drink, and he got a little stoned, you know. He called "Cottontail," and it's a pretty fast tune, and he couldn't play it. And Parker just took over and played the whole thing *perfectly*. Ben's signature tune! So he got a little peed off on that one, and he started looking at us funny. And he's a gigantic guy, Ben Webster. Strong, big guy. Parker says, "Hey, Ben, you better lighten up or you can't play your own music." Well, that did it. He turned around and says, "You two get the hell out of here," and we were fired the second night.

It wasn't just Webster. Bird pulled Stan from one jam session to another, carving older musicians to pieces, leaving them shaken and suddenly insecure. He was the only Bird in a roomful of cats, fluttering near the upper limits, out of reach.

The boppers were so confident that they sometimes showed overt contempt for the audience. Turning away from the crowd while soloing and not acknowledging applause became part of the bebop repertoire. Many boppers disdained the gratuitous showmanship of the black minstrel tradition that carried into the swing era. Ralph Ellison bemoaned, "Especially were they resentful of Louis Armstrong, whom . . . they considered an Uncle Tom."

Ellison also regretted bebop's divorce from dancing. Folks came to *listen*. Many older musicians hated it and were publicly derisive of a music that Ellison, their unofficial spokesman, described as "nervous, fragmented, and shrill." Swing era guitarist Eddie Condon famously said, "We don't flat our fifths; we drink 'em."

But, as always, the lines between the genres of jazz were blurry. While Bird was cutting his rivals to ribbons, he was also politicking Buddy Tate to get him into the Count Basie Orchestra. "Man, I'm from Kansas City, and I should be in there," Bird told Tate.

"I know he can play, but he looks so bad," said Basie.

When Tate took Basie to hear Bird, Parker was wearing bright-colored fireman's suspenders and high-water pants. Basie's mind was made up when Bird got sick onstage.

Bird's degeneracy became symbolic of bebop, but less so than Gillespie's positive and playful side. Dizzy's horn-rimmed glasses, goatee, French beret, and inflatable cheeks became iconic during the bebop craze. Boppers spoke their own language and coined the term "hip" ("I call it 'hep,'" said Stan). As it caught on, more listeners could catch the humor in the music. Dizzy never fit the profile of the indignant, poker-faced bopper. He often grinned and goofed as much as Louis Armstrong.

"See, Dizzy was a comedian," said trumpeter Howard McGhee. "He's funny, he likes to be funny and laugh and so forth. Bird wasn't like that. He was a serious man. And he figured, when you hit that bandstand, you supposed to be serious. You ain't supposed to be making people laugh and all that bullshit, like Dizzy would be doing. And he would get mad when he'd see Dizzy do that."

The two were a study in contrasts for Stan. Dizzy remained married to his devoted and devoutly Catholic wife Lorraine for fifty-four years. Bird was a bigamist who married four times before he was thirty. Aside from an occasional taste of marijuana, Dizzy eschewed drugs completely. While Dizzy invested, Bird borrowed from loan sharks and pawned his saxophone.

The "first all-bebop band" caused a sensation during an eight-week engagement at the Three Deuces Club in 1944. The quintet perfected a repertoire of new music: "Salt

Peanuts," "Confirmation," "Shaw 'Nuff," "Hot House," and other bebop classics. Dizzy called this time with Bird, Stan, Russell, and Haig "the height of the perfection of our music."

At rehearsal, Dizzy says to Bird, "You have to look good, Yard. You can't be embarrassing us wearing those clothes." Parker starts sulking but Dizzy says he's going to buy Bird a new suit. Diz knows better than to give the money to Charlie, so he assigns me to take him shopping because no store is going to let in this raggedy-looking black guy by himself. We get him a nice suit and shoes and a tie. Get his hair cut, and he's looking good.

We rehearsed at the Three Deuces in the afternoon. I still don't have my own drums. Doc Harold West had his set in there, and I used his. Diz brought in all this new music, and the band immediately jelled. Within thirty minutes, it was together. It was a perfect package. Al Haig was incredible.

We opened in the Three Deuces, and everything broke loose. You couldn't get in the door. It was like that for the whole eight weeks. I couldn't wait to go to work each night. I'd go an hour early and just sit. This band is on fire, I want to tell you. We never had an off night. That band was tremendous.

Word was out that the Three Deuces quintet was the hippest band in the nation, and celebrities like Tallulah Bankhead, Elizabeth Taylor, Burgess Meredith, and Frank Sinatra showed up over the course of the engagement. But the most auspicious fan at the Three Deuces was a young Miles Davis. He would later rule jazz, but at the time, Miles was a Juilliard student fresh from St. Louis.

Miles Davis was cocky. Always dressed in a Brooks Brothers suit with all three buttons buttoned and standing around the Three Deuces when we were there with a matchbook, copying down chord changes. He was walking this hip sort of strut, sort of a bent over shuffle, and he always had his trumpet in his leather case.

One day on a break, we're at the Three Deuces and Miles comes back and he's cocky, you know. He goes up to Dizzy and says, "I can play anything you can play," and Dizzy smiles and says, "Yeah, but an octave lower." Miles was a smart mouth. We were always telling him, "Shut up, Junior, you don't know what you're talking about."

When Bird formed a new band after the Three Deuces gig, he hired both Stan and Miles for a two-month engagement at the Spotlite Club. The Spotlite Sextet included Bud Powell or George Wallington on piano, Curly Russell or Leonard Gaskin on bass, Dexter Gordon on tenor saxophone, and Max Roach alternating on drums. Again, Stan found himself at the center of jazz history, anchoring the union of Charlie Parker and Miles Davis. Stan and Miles became fast friends and were soon sharing an apartment after Stan, in search of a little sanity, flew the Bird's nest. According to Davis, he and Stan did a couple of stints under the same roof. "I came back to New York in high spirits," the trumpeter wrote in his autobiography. "I didn't have my own place, so I stayed with Stan Levey until I could get back on my feet. Stan and I had lived together for a while in 1945, so we were good friends."

Davis eventually became an international star who complemented his public persona with photo shoots of himself working out in the ring with sparring partners. Miles was in awe of Jack Johnson and Sugar Ray Robinson, but it was his roommate Stan Levey who first took Miles to the gym and taught him a thing or two.

Meanwhile, Bird was doing the teaching at the Spotlite.

"I learned so much about phrasing from Bird," Stan recalled. "That may sound funny coming from a drummer. But the way he played alto saxophone indicated how I should shape time and structure my solos. Every time he played, he gave me a lesson."

Dexter Gordon echoed Stan's sentiments. "Crash course?" he said. "Oh, yeah! Because I never knew what he was gonna call. Nobody else did, either. It was the time when he started playing all these sophisticated standards . . . sometimes Miles just stood there, open-mouthed. We all did."

I hadn't seen Bird for days, and I just took my meager belongings and moved in with Miles near Central Park West. Old brownstones. Billie Holiday, Dexter Gordon, Sarah Vaughan—they all lived there near us. Freddie Webster, a fine trumpet player. He was on the same floor. It was a musical enclave and we all got along beautifully, and there was some good music that came out of that. It was like the gym in Philly, with me the only white face.

Wherever I was playing, Miles goes down with me. We were very good friends. I used to take him to the gym—Stillman's or Sugar Ray Robinson's—and work out with him, teach him a few things, get him on the bag, you know. He was as open to me as he was closed to his audience. He always made himself hard-edged, and I always got the feeling that he wasn't, really, and he didn't want to show that soft edge. You can hear it in his playing. If you just listen, you can hear it.

His father was the richest dentist—black dentist—in St. Louis. He had his own horses and acres and acres of land.

Miles had walking-around money. His father was wealthy enough to support him and send him to school.

One thing about Miles, he wouldn't bathe. Oh, he'd spruce up and look razor-sharp in the Brooks Brothers suits his father bought him, but he's a brat, see, and unless his mother kicks his ass, he doesn't bother to take a bath. I had to kick his ass to get him in there, the bathroom down the hall.

But Miles admonished me, too, for using. Dexter and I would shoot up together in front of Miles. He didn't like it. Not then.

About six months I lived there with Miles and all those other musicians. Freddie Webster ended up getting pushed out of the top floor of a building in Chicago. They found him dead in the street, broken up bad.

Among the many participants in the apartment enclave scene was Billie Holiday. Stan was in awe of her gorgeous features and her inimitable vocal styling. Holiday knew Stan was part of "the club" and felt at ease in his company, sometimes asking him to escort her home after a gig or while on a mission to score. Stan remembered her as rarely gregarious, but always open. Stan also sat in with her onstage and experienced first-hand her command of a room.

"When she appeared, the room would go dark," said Stan. "The silence was deafening. She had an aura. Total control without even opening her mouth."

Drummer Roy Battle confirmed, "They would turn off all the air conditioning, they wouldn't serve anything, the waitress wouldn't take any orders, everything came to a standstill. And she would just come on and just be Billie. It was that she was the queen."

CHAPTER 6

CALIFORNIA

One of the jobs I had during this time was subbing for Davey Tough in Woody Herman's band at the Hotel Pennsylvania on Thirty-Fourth Street and Seventh Avenue. Davey Tough did whatever he wanted with that band. This little guy could take the band and turn it upside down and inside out if he wanted. I couldn't figure out where the power and energy were coming from. I kept looking for a second drummer. Shelly Manne was in the navy and he was always around Fifty-Second Street in his uniform. He and I took turns sitting in for Davey, and we became good friends. Sometimes it was as much as three times a week, because Davey was an epileptic *and* an alcoholic.

Towards the end of the Three Deuces gig, I got a call from Woody's manager. Davey, who was one of my idols, fell off the stage and got hurt pretty bad, so he was out and they wanted me to finish out the tour. It was big money: two hundred and fifty dollars a week! I was making fifty-six a week with Dizzy. I went to Dizzy and said, "Man, what should I do?" Dizzy said, "Go make the bread. We'll get Max to finish out, and your job will be here when you get back."

It was another coup for Stan. Herman's was the number-one band in the nation at the time, surpassing even Benny

Goodman in record sales and fan polls. The band featured excellent young musicians like brothers Pete and Conte Candoli, Billy Bauer, Chubby Jackson, and Flip Phillips. Sitting serendipitously in the trombone chair was Bill Harris, Stan's old gasman from West Philly. Woody's principal arranger was Neal Hefti, a singular talent whose future would intertwine with Stan's on the boyish, hyperactive *Batman* theme, which Hefti composed and Stan played on.

Woody Herman was the premier jazz musician to come out of Milwaukee. Born to a German father and a Polish mother, Herman cut his musical teeth in 1920s Chicago, where gangsters shot him in the leg after a night listening to Earl Hines at Al Capone's Grand Terrace Ballroom.

"We were in the Grand Terrace Ballroom," remembered Herman. "Somebody spotted that Fuzzy had a big diamond on his finger . . . and we were tipping everybody like it was going out of style, so they figured us for live ones . . . We got about a block when we were stopped by a traffic light. A big black sedan drove up . . . three guys jumped out. One of them had a gun . . . the one with a gun shot into the floorboards, and my leg happened to be in the way."

Herman was already a swing-era legend when Stan joined, but his best days were ahead of him. By surrounding himself with younger musicians and playing original compositions by none other than Dizzy Gillespie, Herman was positioning himself in the vanguard of the post-war big bands. Stan came in at a transitional time. As a bebop drummer steeped in Gillespie, Stan was a bridge to Woody's famous "Thundering Herd," which featured Stan Getz, Al Cohn, and Zoot Sims in a saxophone section that became one of the most celebrated in jazz.

So I went up to Minneapolis, very excited but also scared. I still couldn't read music and I still don't have any drums—not even a cymbal. I played on Davey Tough's set.

Now, for the first time since the few days with Goodman, it's five shows a day in a theater. It's very different. With Dizzy and Charlie, it's more intuitive playing—fast—*papapapapapapapa*. But with the big band, it's slower, swingy, more patterns to catch with the brass, more head work, laying for the figures, things like that. Ralph Burns and Neal Hefti were writing those great charts. The arrangements were just outstanding. I just absorb this new thing, the lights and theaters and one-nighters and big buses and money.

Woody was a taskmaster, but he never asked if I could read music. I faked it, turning the pages. The band was so fantastic, it didn't really need a drummer.

One night during a show, Woody says to me, "Pick up the fly swatters!" "Huh? What?" I didn't know what he was talking about until someone told me, "He means the brushes, Stan."

Everyone in the band loved him, but he had an aggressive streak, and at that time, he drank a lot. He'd pour a drink over a guy's head, but with a laugh and a smile. Playing with Woody was great. Having that experience made it possible for me to play in other big bands during the next few years when I spent short periods with Freddie Slack, Charlie Ventura, Georgie Auld, and Boyd Raeburn, who had sort of an avant-garde orchestra.

I was with Woody Herman for two or three months. That cleaned me up until the first day I got back to New York, then bang—back to six capsules a day.

Touring with Woody Herman was a great experience for Stan, but it came with a drawback. Shortly after the Three Deuces gig, Dizzy Gillespie had the opportunity to take the quintet into the studio and record for the Guild label in May of 1945. With Stan on tour with Woody Herman and Max Roach on the road with Benny Carter, Dizzy hired a swing hero of Stan's named Big Sid Catlett. The sessions went down in history as the first pure bebop recordings.

I'm really sorry I missed those. I should've been on that record. To this day, I could kick my ass. But I thought Sid did a wonderful job, and he's still one of my heroes. I had met him the year before, and he showed me some tricks. Sid was a pussycat. The guy had beautiful stick control. He showed me how to control the sticks better by snapping them up after each down stroke.

"Use the bounce, the momentum of the down stroke," he told me, "and flick the stick up after each down stroke." He knew how to keep the sticks moving, and he knew exactly how to use the set and the cymbals. That session showed how versatile he was and what he was capable of doing.

After his stint with Woody Herman, Stan moved into a rooming house for eight dollars a week and jammed around Manhattan with Charlie Parker. Stan credited his flexibility as a drummer to the need to adapt to varying conditions and limited resources. "You had to sit down and play on any piece of crap that happened to be available," he said. "I never had my own drums, and I learned to make do with anything."

"I remember dropping in on Stan one night in Tin Pan Alley," said bassist Phil Leshin. "The drummer got up and Stan sat down in the middle of a tune. The tempo was way up there, a difficult pulse to hold. He never missed a beat. He was playing on the ride cymbal, right-handed. Suddenly he felt uncomfortable with the set-up and switched everything around—cymbal, high hat, bass drum, the whole thing, without losing the time feeling. Stan always amazed me with his facility, his adaptability."

Stan's next big adventure started when Dizzy called and said, "Get ready, Stanley. We're going to California. You, Bird, Al Haig, and a new bass player I found in Detroit. I got us an eight-week engagement at Billy Berg's in Los Angeles."

Billy Berg offered mainstream entertainment, but he was always open and eager for the latest thing—in this case, the so-called "bebop" that was making a splash in New York. Outside of a small group of black musicians working on Central Avenue, bebop was still unknown in Los Angeles, and Berg was keen to offer it before anyone else.

A new bass player? I was stunned. Curly and I had worked together beautifully. We had the camaraderie and the musical interaction. We took those furious tempos and laid 'em off on each other. I would carry the whole thing with the horns and then with the piano, and Curly'd pick up and I would get some blood back in my hands, just lay back a little, you know.

But Dizzy insists the guy's dynamite, and it's Dizzy's band. We don't rehearse before getting on the train, and this kid is pretty cocky. I'm worried the whole ride out.

The young bassist was Ray Brown, and he came to the band with his best friend, a vibraphonist and fellow Motor City cat named Milt Jackson. Jackson's vibraphone was as pitiable as Bird's horn, requiring restringing after every set.

Stan's drum kit consisted of one ride cymbal and whatever set of traps he could borrow once he arrived in Los Angeles. Dizzy had to hire tenor saxophonist Lucky Thompson to cover for Bird's inevitable absences. Such was the condition of the ragtag crew of musical sophisticates eagerly anticipated in California.

We get to Chicago, where we had a ten-hour layover, and Dizzy says, "Come on Stan, let's go see Louis Armstrong."

So we go over to his hotel. We walk in, and Louis is sitting there with about two or three people buzzing around him—manicuring his feet, conking his hair, rubbing him down—and he's smoking a huge marijuana joint! I mean a real bomber!

He looks at me and he freezes—you know—the way his eyes bug out. He says, "Oh man, Dizzy! Why you bringing him in here?" He thought I was a detective! I was big, you know, working out, boxing—and I was wearing a hat and an overcoat. He thought I was a cop. God knows what he's thinking. I can't go back in his mind, but maybe he's paranoid that Dizzy brought the police to get him busted so Dizzy could be the next big trumpet man, who knows? He never believed that I was a musician. "This is my drummer!" Dizzy kept saying, but Louis just said, "I don't believe that shit."

We got back on the train, and Charlie's a mess. He's halfway to hell. He can't get any dope in Chicago, so he drinks like crazy. He passes out and pretty soon we see a yellow river come flowing down the aisle. Parker pissed himself and he doesn't even know it. He's a basket case.

Later on, we're in the middle of the desert and the train stops to take on water from a huge tank out in the middle of nowhere. I'm looking out the window and I see something moving out in the distance. I look closely and it's Charles Parker out there with his horn, walking away from the train.

"Dizzy! I think you better see this! Your saxophonist is wandering off into the desert!"

He says, "Well, Stan, you're his friend, you better go get him."

I'm thinking, "Well, it's *your* band," but I go out there and catch up with him. "Bird! What the hell are you doing out here?"

"I'm gonna go get me something. I gotta get straight."

He was almost in a coma. His eyes up in his head, mumbling. So I drag him back to the train. Suppose I didn't see him? I could've been on the other side of the train. He would've died out there. Nobody could do anything for him. What are you gonna do? Poor bastard. What do you do with a child?

The train pulls in a couple of days before the engagement. Palm trees, perfect weather, everything looks clean and beautiful—but Dizzy's livid. He has a major problem on his hands. We drag Bird to a colored hotel in the Japanese section called the Downtown House. Never forget it. We all check in, we sit Bird down, we make some calls and some guy comes up with this Mexican stuff they had out here called "mud"—an unrefined opium. You had to filter it through cotton because it had twigs and dirt in it. It was awful, just awful. Am I being too graphic with this? Just terrible. It's good enough to get him together, but nothing more. I stopped chasing it, once I got out there. I was mostly clean from my time with Woody Herman, and I wasn't touching that filthy stuff.

We went to rehearse with the new guys and I'm still worried about playing with a new bassist. Dizzy beats off a very fast tune. We're flying along and I hear this *great* bass sound coming through which I'd never heard before. Every

note was clear as a bell, and the tempos were *right* there.
I looked at him and we grinned at each other. Ray Brown.
Great, great bass player.

We were a mixed bag of nuts. We hired the men's room
attendant at Billy Berg's to provide our transportation to
the club. He had a 1930 Plymouth Coupe with a long, long
trunk. Two of us had to lie in the trunk on blankets. The
Downtown House was a rattrap. People fighting, getting
beat up. After a few weeks, I was sick of it and I was sick of
riding in the trunk, so I moved into the Drake Hotel where
Al Haig was living.

To the average customer off the street, the music was too
fast and too squeaky. "Where's the singer?" was a question
to which "Salt Peanuts" was the wise-ass answer. Much of
Berg's clientele came to be entertained by the performers who
were splitting the bill with the beboppers: Harry the Hipster
and Slim "Always Stay Commercial" Gaillard, who got into a
fistfight with Dizzy in the men's room halfway through the
engagement. Many patrons were puzzled not only by the music but by the two white guys playing in a black band.

It was a different story for the West Coast jazz musicians.
Buddy Collette, whom Stan later recorded with, said, "This
was for real. The stuff that you heard on records that you
didn't believe, you . . . had to believe because you saw people
standing there playing it . . . it was kind of scary to hear, because they were playing so fast that we didn't understand what
they were really playing . . . They were using notes that we
didn't even dare to use before because it would be considered
wrong. And those stops and gos between Dizzy and Bird . . .
you know, you'd look at everybody and say, 'Can you believe
what we just heard?'"

Among the cats coming to Berg's practically every night were Howard McGhee, Hampton Hawes, and Charles Mingus, who described Stan in his autobiography as an "ofay" and a "Jew boy" who "sure can play!"

Mingus came in every night. Him and Ray Brown would do some duos. Mingus was nuts then. He was completely crazy. Not vicious, but I mean, you know, a little screwy. But most of the musicians who came couldn't get near that bandstand. They wouldn't dare. I mean, they couldn't handle it. Couldn't do it.

A lot of movie stars came: Ava Gardner, Mickey Rooney, Jennifer Jones. It became sort of a legendary engagement. We did a radio broadcast every night and somebody has a wire recording of that, every broadcast. Someone out there has that.

We did a record date, out in Glendale at the Trinity Broadcasting Studio for Ross Russell on Dial Records. Bird doesn't show up. No one sees him for the last three or four days, and when it's time to go to the airport, he's gone. Dizzy gave me twenty bucks and a cab and said, "See if you can find him." I looked everywhere—all the jungle places. Couldn't find him. So I leave the ticket at the hotel desk, and we fly back. Twenty-one stops from Burbank to New York. We find out later Bird came and got the ticket, but what does he do? Hocks it for dope.

Bird crept out of the underworld long enough to do his own sessions for Dial, only to sign half the royalties over to his supplier, an L.A. pusher known as Moose the Mooche. One night, Bird, wearing nothing but a pair of socks, wandered repeatedly into the hotel lobby, looking for change for a quarter.

The staff kept bouncing him back to his room, which was soon engulfed in smoke and crackling with flames from a fire that Bird started, presumably by passing out with a cigarette.

The fire trucks came and they put a net on him and that was it. Took him downtown. Judge committed him to [Camarillo State Mental Hospital]. Stayed there about six months.

Back in New York, we went into the Spotlite Club on Fifty-Second Street with Dizzy, and instead of Bird we had Leo Parker on baritone. And we also had a certain famous saxophonist—a snitch whose name I don't like to mention—in that band.

We did four weeks there at the Spotlite, and then Dizzy got his big band together and I couldn't be a part of it, because with the big band he had to tour through the South, and he said it wouldn't work, a mixed band. "I wouldn't want to put you through that, Stanley," he said.

I understood, but when I heard the band, they were out of tune. I didn't like the band. It wasn't the quality of what we'd just finished. It was really raggedy. I didn't think much of the drummer, Teddy Stewart. I said, "Man, I could do better than this."

But for a while there was a movement to get the white guys out of the music. "You're stealing our music, getting more jobs." I guess I'm the wrong color. We called it Crow Jim. Curly Russell—I went down to see him play with Art Blakey. "Hi Curly, how ya doing?"

Nothing.

Regardless of the reasons, Stan did face a scarcity of work after his time with Gillespie. He reverted to boxing, as well as some other even more dangerous pursuits.

I was living in Brooklyn, working sporadically, running with druggies, and using heavy. I even did some boxing in those days, if you can believe that. I was able to keep in shape somehow. I fought at Turner's Arena in D.C. and at the old Garden in New York, at about Fiftieth and Eighth. Make a little money, that's all. In D.C., an older guy broke my jaw and it was wired up for six weeks, so that took care of that.

There were some Irish bars over there by the old Garden—Ryan's, Kelly's. I hung out there, leading a sort of dual life. Some tough guys hung out there. Real thugs. I met a few young guys like me. These two guys, we got friendly. I knew they were into some heavy stuff. They asked me, "You looking to make a little money? We're going to do something, and we could use you to drive." I knew it was illegal, but I didn't know what they were doing, and I didn't ask.

They show up in what turns out to be a stolen LaSalle. I drive them up Broadway. They get out and tell me not to move, keep the motor running and they'll be right back. I still don't know what's going on, but a few minutes later they come walking back nice and easy with a bag. They get in and say, "Hit it." I find out later they hit a box office.

We go down to about Eleventh, pull over and park. They tell me, "Get rid of the keys. We'll see you tomorrow at the bar." And they did. Four hundred dollars they paid me. And we did it again. Another box office. Twice I drove for those guys, but after that I said, "I'm in over my head." You're looking at twenty-five years with that kind of stuff.

A trumpet player by the name of Sonny Rich got me into the business of selling magazines door to door. I did pretty well, you know. Cold call—knock on the door. One time, I found an open door and I grabbed some jewelry. All this

is raunchy stuff. Junky stuff. I don't like to talk about it. The
maid saw me and I got arrested.

In 1948, Stan and Bird were reunited through Norman
Granz's *Jazz at the Philharmonic*. Granz was a promoter and
record company entrepreneur who staged boisterous jam sessions inside concert halls all over the country. His concept was
to capture the spirit and competition of the jam sessions for
large-scale, commercial consumption.

"I like my musicians to be friends offstage," Granz said.
"But when they're onstage, I want blood." Audiences respond-
ed by egging the cats on with whistles and raucous outbursts
of encouragement. "*Go cat, go!*"

It was a formula that made Granz rich, but the impresario
had other motives as well. Appalled by racism and segregation, Granz viewed jazz as the perfect vehicle by which to fight
inequality. His interracial troupes of musicians challenged segregation in hotels, restaurants, and concert halls, and Granz
sometimes took a loss by refusing to play for segregated
audiences.

Granz employed many of the best swing-era musicians, but
he was also an early proponent of bebop, and he invited artists
like Stan and Bird to fan the flames of his fiery performances.
The two old roommates were tight again after Parker's extended stay at Camarillo, but to nobody's surprise, Bird was back
on the mooch.

We did a countrywide tour: Chicago, St. Louis, Kansas City,
Boston, Buffalo . . . We'd all show up in the lobby, and a
lot of, you know, throat clearing, and Norman would say,
"This is our group. Let's have our rooms." He was terrific.
Norman really broke a lot of barriers. We just showed up:

"Here we are."

The rhythm section on that tour was Duke Jordan, Tommy Potter, and me. We stayed on the whole time, playing behind Charlie Parker, Barney Kessel, Lester Young, Sarah Vaughan, Jimmy Jones, Red Rodney, Dexter Gordon. Twenty-five dollars a night.

I was out on bail on that jewelry case, and my lawyer screwed up and I was on the calendar a day too soon. I went to Norman at the Sherman Hotel in Chicago. I says, "Norman, I gotta go, man, I gotta go."

"Whaddya mean you gotta go?"

"I gotta be in court tomorrow."

He starts ranting and raving. "Look, Norman, just pay me what you owe me and give me the ticket you owe me."

"I ain't givin' ya nothin'!"

He wouldn't budge. Norman hated guys who used drugs.

Well, I dumped him. Knocked him out cold and took exactly what he owed me out of his wallet.

What am I gonna do? I had to get out of there. He owed me the money. What really upset me was that I had Shelly Manne available, right there in Chicago.

So I got what he owed me but I still needed some more money, so I went to the least likely guy in the world to lend anyone money—Charlie Parker, of all people. He goes into his own pocket and lent me money. Never been done before in the history of the world. *But . . .* he wanted the drum set I had borrowed for the tour as security. He makes me sign a promissory note.

Now I leave. I get on the bus—I'm depressed—and I go back to New York. What I didn't know was that back in Chicago, Bird was trying to hock the drums! Somehow Red Rodney kept it from happening. He stood behind Bird at the pawnshop and motioned for the guy not to make a deal.

In 1947, Stan married Shirley Van Dyke, a roller-skating jitterbug champion with ambitions of stardom who endeared herself to musicians and actors with calculating charm, engaging in the business of a lady of the night.

"I have no idea how they met," said Stan's oldest son, Robert. "My mom was a beautiful lady, but I also think my old man felt sorry for her."

Shirley also got hooked on the same injections that enslaved Stan.

"They were both heroin addicts," said Robert. "They were living that life."

Robert Levey was born on February 6, 1948. Stan lifted him in and out of his crib and performed other fatherly functions for about a year before he and Shirley divorced. Not long after, Shirley and young Robert moved to Los Angeles with the assistance of Frank Sinatra.

"Somehow she had a connection with Sinatra," said Robert. "She went into treatment—put me in foster care—and got off heroin . . . looking beautiful. Sinatra said, 'I'll get you in the movie business, fly you out here and help get you started.' That's when I met him, at the opening of *The Man with the Golden Arm*. He escorted us to our seats and I shook his hand. She took the stage name Shirley Francis, after Sinatra. She thought he was going to marry her . . . so she starts drinking, and it's all downhill from there.

"She was very sick. She did beat me. Broke a clothes hanger over my back. She told me she had more than a few abortions. That's how destructive she was. I was the only one. Nobody could live with my mother. She was very emotionally disturbed. My old man told me she once put out a cigarette on his face."

After they divorced, Stan tried never to speak Shirley's name again.

In 1949, Stan played with saxophonist Stan Getz for the first time, in vibraphonist Terry Gibbs's band. Having worked so closely with Bird, Stan had a reverence for the saxophone and high standards for players; aside from Parker, Getz had the biggest impression on Stan as a saxophonist.

"Stan was in the first band I ever had," Gibbs remembered. "We played two weeks at Soldier Meyers' in Brooklyn, following Miles Davis into the place. The front line was Stan Getz, Kai Winding, and myself. The rhythm section was Stan, George Wallington, and Curly Russell. Stan was taken off the job. He had some trouble because he didn't have a union card. Hadn't paid his dues, or something like that."

But Stan was in the band long enough to make an impression on Getz, who hired the drummer for his first record date on the Prestige label later that same year. Al Haig played piano and Gene Ramey, Bird's old friend from K.C., was the bassist on the date.

Stan Getz was quite unknown in those days. We became friends in about '48, and he hired me for a record date and a couple of jobs. Those were his first big sellers. "Long Island Sound" was one of them. Quite a few others. Of course, later he became the bossa nova king.

The two Stans shared more in common than their names, including membership in "The Club." Getz's heroin addiction was so strong he once tried to hold up a Seattle drugstore in a pathetic attempt to scrounge up enough money for a fix. He was caught and sentenced to six months. The whole debacle was contrary to the man's decent upbringing and to his gorgeous sound, which enraptured listeners all over the world and prompted John Coltrane to say, "Let's face it—we'd all sound like that if we could."

> When Getz and I were both hooked in a bad way, we were at the American Hotel in New York, shooting up in the men's room. The private detective from the hotel came in, banged on the stall, and said, "All right, you fags! Get outta here!" When we came out, we had to play the part. I said, "*Well*, Stanley, I can *see* we're not wanted in here!" And we sashayed out of there as fast as we could.

Getz would later insert himself into the West Coast jazz scene that Stan Levey came to epitomize in the 1950s, and the two Stans would play together on some classic record dates of that era.

> I think the warmth—the bone, muscle, and blood that's on the mouthpiece—is an extension of the brain and soul. Stan Getz had that. That damn thing was an extension of his being, it really was. I worked with him a lot. I couldn't believe it.

Later in 1949, a mobster named Joseph Catalano sold his Manhattan property at 1678 Broadway to a pair of jazz-loving entrepreneurs named Morris and Irving Levy. The brothers named their new club Birdland in honor of Charlie Parker, who headlined on opening night. The venue seated five hundred people and booked as many as five acts each night. It wasn't long before Birdland eclipsed the clubs on Fifty-Second Street to become "The Jazz Corner of the World." Sugar Ray

Robinson and Joe Louis were regulars, and Jack Kerouac wrote about the club in his seminal work *On the Road*.

One of the first employees the brothers hired was a ravishing young lady named Angela Neylan, who arrived in New York at the tender age of seventeen. As a dancer, Angela had a good ear for music and became enamored with jazz. Her job at Birdland brought her close to most of the major jazz musicians of the time, including Stan Levey.

"I worked at Birdland as a semi-manager for Morris and Irving Levy," Angela said. "Nice young Jewish brothers, good businessmen, but years later I heard that somebody stabbed Irv to death and Morris ended up in prison, of all things. Pee Wee Marquette, who was about three feet tall, stood outside looking like a captain in a bellboy type of uniform, calling people in with that voice of his. One time, Billie Holiday came in with two dogs on a leash—these wolfhound creatures. I couldn't believe my eyes, but she could get away with that sort of thing. Bud Powell was the sharpest dresser. He looked fabulous all the time—Chesterfield coat with wonderful wool and the velvet collar. Dapper! Everything matched, and he was quite handsome. George Wallington was there a lot. He was a lovely piano player and was one of the few who had an actual family that cooked and spent time together. Of course, Miles was always around. Monk never said anything. One time, Stan and I shared a cab with him and about nine hundred other people from Brooklyn to Manhattan. I was feeling silly, and I said to him, 'Don't you ever keep quiet? It's really annoying.' Everybody laughed but him.

"I went with two girlfriends to the Three Deuces, and Stan was there playing with Allen Eager. Stan was sitting at a table with some men in suits—music business types, maybe—and Allen Eager announces over the microphone, "Stanleyyy, we're waaaiting!" Stan said something back that was rather un-musician-like in the sense that it wasn't a hip type of smart aleck response but rather very normal and down-to-earth. I could just tell that he was a nice guy. And I immediately thought he was gorgeous.

"A few nights later, we were at the Royal Roost. They had a place in back they called the bleachers where you could sit and listen and didn't have to order anything. He was sitting cattycorner to me, and he just kept talking to me. At about 3:00 AM, we walked down Broadway to Whalen's drugstore and sat at the counter and talked until it was light. Then he walked me home to my sister's friends. I looked at him and said to myself, 'It's very possible I might marry this person.' For the rest of our lives, it never changed: the rest of the world is there, but that person is your home—like a teepee."

The concept of a loving, committed relationship was as fragile for Angela as it was for Stan. Her own father had run off before she was born, and her mother, Adele Cataldo, had remained single, devoting herself to the full-time job of raising her daughters in an otherwise traditional Italian Catholic household. Stan's own parents never reconciled. Stan's father, David, did remarry, but Angela would never meet him, for later that same year, Dave Levey died from a bullet to the head.

Well, my old man, you know, he committed suicide in '49.

In the used car business, you buy a car and you take the title from the guy, and you take the title up to the finance company—they were called that in those days—and they would finance the title, maybe eighty percent, you know, whatever it was, and you'd have that cash. Then, when you sold the car at a profit, you had to pay off the title to get it, you know what I mean? To give the buyer the title to the car.

> Well, he was screwing around. I think he got about seven
> cars into it, and he couldn't handle it. Blew his brains out.

Arthur Pritz, who worked with Stan on a documentary about his life called *Stan Levey: The Original Original,* said Stan wasn't positive that his father's death was a suicide, only that "he was shot in the head." Considering Dave Levey's crooked ways and mob connections, Stan couldn't help but wonder whether it really was suicide.

Later, Stan learned that Dave and his second wife had a daughter named Joan who was only two years old when Dave died. Stan tried to locate his half-sister, but her last name had changed with adoption and he was never able to find her.

At the time of Dave's death, Stan mostly felt distant and resentful toward his father and did not even attend his funeral. Nevertheless, a decade later, Stan and Angela would name their second son "David."

Angela was initially naive about drugs. "She thought it was like having a drink," said Stan. When his addiction and its implications became more apparent, she begged him to stop. Angela would get her wish—but only after having her devotion tested by a two-year prison sentence.

CHAPTER 7

PRISON AND REDEMPTION

Sonny Stitt was high-strung, always moving fast. "*Heyba-by, heybaby . . .* " He was a shadow. Always paranoid. I'm working in Birdland, and he brings this light-skinned black guy over. Says, "This is my guy . . . my main man from Detroit. Can you pick up something for him on your way?" Gives me twenty dollars. I go out and score, come back. "Here you go." I don't make any money off it.

A month later, I get served with a secret indictment for illegal sale of heroin. The guy was a federal agent. Sonny Stitt had made a deal to save his own skin. He used me as a patsy. You can't get any lower. But as it turned out, Sonny Stitt saved my life. I thank him for it, believe it or not, I do.

I pled guilty. If I went to trial, I'd have got five to ten. The judge—this was my second time in front of him—he said, "If I see you in the system, I'll find you, and I'll come in on the case. I'll put you away for the rest of your life." And he wasn't kidding. Judge Goddard. He didn't like me, but I like him for what he did. He really got through to me. I said, "Judge, this is the last time you see me!" And I meant it. Standing in front of that judge at the sentencing, I made up my mind that dope was over for me.

I got nineteen months, federal prison. I went in on May 10, 1950. Lexington for a year, then I wound up in Fort Worth. I was relieved. It was over. No more hustling for money at five in the morning. I couldn't continue.

As relieved as Stan was to be free from heroin, he was tortured by his separation from Angela and the threat that he might lose her to a free man. Leaving her in the hospital, in the condition she was in, hadn't helped.

"I went to Cornell University Hospital right when Stan was in the middle of the court case," Angela said. "I had spots all over my legs and arms, and bruises. They examined me and from then on, classes and medical students came around ten times a day, looking at me. I didn't know what it was until forty years later, when my son told me it was ITP [idiopathic thrombocytopenic purpura], which means, 'We don't know what the hell it is.'

"Stan would come up and see me. We'd sit on the sun porch and hug and kiss, and we were crying when the day for him to leave came. He said, 'This is it,' and he went off to prison while I was imprisoned in the hospital for more than a month. It was hilarious when I went to leave and they said, 'Here's the bill.' We didn't have two cents. I left the hospital and lugged everything to the bus station and got on a bus to Philadelphia to meet Stan's mother for the first time before going home to Washington. On that bus—this was before ibuprofen—I was experiencing the worst pains of my life, maybe worse than childbirth. It was so horrible, my legs, my arms, my back. It was atrocious.

"I got to Philadelphia and went to [Stan's mother] Essie's work at a department store and there she was, looking marvelous. We took a cab to her apartment and on the way there, we stopped off and she got out of the cab near what I presume was a liquor store and came back out with a paper bag. She lived with her mother, Mary Hoffman, who was so cute. Grandma Hoffman didn't approve of anybody—including me, I don't think—but she was a darling Jewish lady: roly-poly, always cooking, with an accent. Wonderful. We talked, and Grandma Hoffman went to bed and it was just Essie and I. And she ended up flat on her back!

"Here I am, a nice Catholic girl with manners. I wasn't about to go to bed and leave her on the floor. If it were today, I certainly would, but not then. I was *pulling* and *dragging* and holding her up and sitting on the floor with her leaning on me. Trying to get her to move. I mean it was just awful, so that just illustrated to me what she did every night and why Stan was so upset about it."

Angela's own mother, Adele, was glad when she learned that Stan was in prison. Someone mixed up with drugs was the worst possible choice for her daughter, not to mention that he was Jewish. So long as she was under Adele Cataldo's roof, Angela was forbidden from corresponding with Stan. Furthermore, Adele had a nice Italian boy in mind for her daughter—Spencer Sinatra, a tenor saxophone player who was the son of one of Adele's good friends. The two mothers conspired with dinner invitations and other arrangements. Adele even went so far as to publish a pre-engagement announcement in the newspaper, which infuriated Angela.

"Poor thing," said Angela about the young man. "It was not good for him. I did my best to convey that I was latched onto something else, but his hopes were up. Stan sent me a letter and told me where I could write him, and I realized that it was just luck that my mother didn't see it. We didn't write very much. She eventually saw one letter and insisted I leave, so I went to live with two girlfriends. Much later, in California, Stan and I went to hear Kenton—this was after Stan had left the band. It was very uncomfortable. Spencer Sinatra was there on the stage, playing tenor in the band."

Withdrawal is beyond hell. In prison, they call it the cement cure. You lay on the cement. You live or die. Now, if you're going to die, the guard says, "Hurry up and die. We need the room." They do. I swear to God. You can't even describe it. You're running from every opening in your body. Cramps. You can't walk. Every nerve end is pulsing and hurting.

But it ends!

I worked on the crazy ward the first six months, holding down these crazy bastards. We used to hold 'em down for the electric shock, you know. These guys were violent—take three, four, five of us to hold 'em down and get 'em back to their room. They used the big guys for that.

They had weights and boxing. All the bags there. Three meals a day. I was at home, man. They kept begging for me to join the prison band, but I didn't want to hear it, see it—don't talk to me about music! That's what got me here. I don't want anything to do with it! I didn't play a lick. Not one beat or nothin'.

Angela's mother was pressuring her—and rightly so—to get away from me. I learned how to pray in prison, praying for her to be there when I got out. Angela told me, "If you ever start that stuff again, I'm gone. You'll never see or talk to me again."

I put in for the farm and boy, I loved it. Worked in the slaughterhouse. I slaughtered cows. I slaughtered pigs. Disemboweled 'em. Wore the boots up to here. We would cook up a steak right there at the slaughterhouse. I graduated to the farm and took care of eighty acres. Get up in the morning at 6:00 AM. I had my own tractor. It was the greatest time of my life up to that point. Gorgeous, beautiful country—Kentucky. It was healthy—my mind was working. I'd drive in for lunch, go back out again . . . they'd have to come out and get me.

So I was in great shape, plus I boxed there. They had all the gear, all the bags. Some colored guys did, too, pretty good boxers. We put on shows, boxing shows. We're not looking to hurt each other. Put on a good show, you know.

I became a different person. I developed a personality which I think I still have today. All the layers I sloughed off, I got rid of. I said, "I'm gonna leave this bag of garbage right here!" I didn't have a psychiatrist. I learned to be a man on the farm. I walked out like a man, with ten dollars.

Stan went back to Philadelphia and moved back in with his mother, but not before stopping in Washington D.C. to see Angela. His prison prayers were answered with her embrace, and he presented her with a promise in the form of his jailhouse tattoo. Covering the scar tissue on the inside of his left elbow was the name "Angela." The cursive of the artist's needle followed the tracks of so many previous punctures to create an impenetrable barrier should Stan ever point a needle there again. To pierce her name would be unthinkable.

Unfortunately, the two would have to carry on a long-distance relationship until Stan could get back on his feet. With Stan in Philly and Angela employed full-time at the Casino Royale nightclub in D.C., their time together was often limited to a couple of hours in a coffee shop. But Stan did get a chance to spend some extra time in D.C. when Charlie Parker called to say he wanted Stan back in his band.

It was risky business. Playing with the very man who had hooked him was the one sure way to fall off the wagon, and Stan knew it. But his resolve to stay clean was strong, and he knew Bird would be playing in D.C. after some Philly dates. So in the spring of 1952, Stan joined up with Parker, Kenny Dorham on trumpet, Walter Bishop Jr. on piano, and Teddy Kotick on bass.

All that time—the nineteen months I was away—I never once touched a drumstick. I came out, and it was like I hadn't missed a day. In early '52, I played some Philly and D.C. dates at the Howard Theater with Charlie Parker, but I really couldn't be around Bird at that time and I cut it short.

My buddy Joe Widra, who I first met at the Downbeat Club when I was there working with Dizzy, he had a record store in downtown Philly and he let me work there. Joe's nickname was "No Eyes," because he had two slits for eyes. We saw, for two weeks, a couple of feds following us. We saw them, and they knew we saw them.

Later, Stan would find out the extent to which the feds were keeping track of him. He didn't know it at the time, but he was on the radar of the top narcotics man in the nation: Harry J. Anslinger, commissioner of the Federal Bureau of Narcotics.

But at the time, Stan was more interested in finding work than worrying about narcotics agents. With Joe Widra's help, Stan became a bandleader.

Joe knew all the club owners. He got me a job playing at the Rendezvous Club. I put together the house band and pretty soon, we were the best house band in Philly. Everyone from

New York—all the singers—wanted us to back them when they came to town. The band was Richie Kamuca on tenor, Nelson Boyd on bass, and Red Garland on piano.

It was fitting that Philly's favorite house band featured two boxers. Like Stan, Red Garland had a prior career in the ring, and in 1942, the pianist survived eight punishing rounds against Sugar Ray Robinson.

Red might have come up short against the great Sugar Ray, but he earned himself a prominent position in jazz history, largely as a result of his work with Miles Davis's first great quintet. By the time they joined forces in Philadelphia, Red and Stan had both retired from boxing, Even so, Stan found himself falling back on his fists shortly after getting out of prison.

My old friend Erroll Garner came to Philly with his band and I went to his hotel to pay a visit. I get up there and Shadow Wilson says, "Come on, baby, I got some good stuff." He starts unwrapping it, and I dumped him. I unloaded on him, hit him right in the face. I didn't mean to, but it was automatic. He thought he was doing me a favor. I helped him up, apologized to him and Erroll.

And then, a couple of weeks later . . . who comes to town?

Sonny Stitt.

Joe Widra says, "Let's go do a number on him," and he goes in there with me. Place called the Showboat. I was big and strong from prison, and Joe looks like an ape. He's like Marciano. It's the kind of place where the bar's in the round and the band plays in the middle. We walk in and we don't sit down. We just stand there and stare right into his face.

You ever seen a charcoal briquette when it's cooking? That's the color he turned. Gray. If there was a skylight, he'd a jumped through the ceiling to escape. He knew he was gonna die that night. Joe stares at him through his slits and I'm mouthing every curse and slur and threat I can think of. Then we leave.

What I heard was he didn't show up the next night for work.

But that wasn't the last I'd seen of Sonny Stitt.

Stan's quartet was called on to back Ella Fitzgerald, Sarah Vaughan, and even non-jazz acts like Burl Ives. They were adaptable to any vocalist, and they swung like hell on their own. Stan's hometown house band was a source of pride and the starting point for the long relationship Stan enjoyed with Richie Kamuca, the Filipino Philly tenor man whose career trajectory followed Stan's for the rest of the decade. Stan became to Richie what Dizzy had been to him: a big brother figure and musical mentor. Twelve years Stan's junior, Kamuca later played on most of Stan's own records and even became godfather to both of Stan and Angela's sons.

CHAPTER 8

ARTISTRY IN RHYTHM

B efore Phil Specter and before the Grateful Dead, there was a "Wall of Sound" in the form of the Stan Kenton Orchestra. Propelled by Stan Levey's drumming, Kenton's band—all nineteen pieces of it—had the loudest, most daring, and explosive sound on the scene. Kenton attached grandiose labels like "progressive jazz" and "neophonic" to his music, terms that engendered loyalty and enthusiasm from an international fan base but derision from many critics who found Kenton's music laborious and bombastic. As the leader of an all-white big band in a post-bop world, Kenton came to symbolize the music's Caucasian—i.e. less authentic—side. Born in Kansas, the registered Republican seemed as square as Bird and Diz were hip, and his music was often pegged with the dreaded jazz criticism, "It doesn't swing."

But Kenton wasn't interested in playing Count Basie charts. Few would deny that Kenton's music wasn't sometimes stiff and overbearing, but his bands were also capable of knocking the socks off even their harshest critics. Intrepid and experimental, Kenton was adding some of the nation's most creative players to his orchestra in the early 1950s. Stan Levey was part of a rebuilding that brought in star soloists like Lee Konitz, Zoot

Sims, and the hilarious Frank Rosolino, a trombone star who told as many jokes as he played notes. Innovative arrangements by Gerry Mulligan, Bill Russo, and Stan's friend Bill Holman sharpened the band onto the cutting edge of modern music.

Kenton's personality seemed as multi-faceted as his music. The bandleader's buttoned-down reputation was counter-balanced by his experimental streak and eccentricities, like his obsession with psychoanalysis. These traits projected the image of a mad scientist, his orchestra a large and very loud laboratory.

Stan Kenton came to Philadelphia for a big engagement at a big club. I knew he had a pretty interesting band. Conte Candoli and other guys in the band, friends of mine, they wanted me in there, so they bring me back and introduce me. He's very impressive when you meet him—about six-foot-four and very well-spoken. I was really impressed with him. He knew I had been in prison and he just looked at me and says, "Are you okay?" I said, "Yeah, I'm okay." That's a great guy. He took a chance on me, you know.

I went right on the bus and hit the road. My starting salary was a hundred and seventy-five dollars a week. I think the highest-paid guy was Maynard Ferguson, who made two hundred dollars.

First we went to Cleveland for a week, which was great because my friend Ellis Tollin moved there after New York and opened a big drum store. Ellis got me a set of drums and sponsorships from Ludwig and Zildjian, so now I finally have my first drum set. I played Ludwig my whole career. To me, they were the best drums. They had the best wood—very mellowed, and kiln-dried. They were very generous. Sticks, anything I needed, Ludwig just sent it out on the road. Later,

I used Regal tip sticks—7A size. Oak—until you couldn't get actual oak anymore. Nylon-tipped. The bass pedal I used was a "Speed King," a famous Ludwig pedal. My cymbal stands were also Ludwig.

The guy before me just couldn't cut it. He later became a very fine drummer, but at that time he didn't have what it took. Kenton went through a lot of drummers because the instrumentation would overpower them. They had some lazy players. Bunch of young, laid-back guys from California. I wanted to go in and swing their ass. Stan moved out a lot of dead wood, and Zoot and Lee Konitz and Frank Rosolino, they all joined about the same time I did, or right after. Bill Holman was writing incredible charts. He writes in lines rather than in solid sounds. His is a linear style. What I mean is, some of Bill's things come out like solos, even though it's really ensemble playing.

People waited for that band to come to their town. We were celebrated. We'd get asked for autographs all the time. The adulation was enjoyable, particularly coming from where I came from—the farm, you know.

Stan was a taskmaster. He would not put up with any drugs. Musically, he was a very open guy. He'd experiment and allow each of his musicians to rise to his level—go as far as you could with whatever you could do. If he thought you were overstepping your abilities, he'd cut you off at that point. But Stan never stopped a guy from progressing and growing musically. I got some very good reading experience. The arrangers wrote in different time signatures—7/4, 5/4, things like that. It was a step up in learning.

In a way, it was an avant-garde band, and it was a very loud orchestra, very ponderous. I never came across anything quite like it. You had to have a boxer's mentality to approach it. I almost had to start working out with weights to keep up with it.

The band got better, and by 1953, it was dynamite. We went to Europe and tore up the whole place. Did fifty-five concerts in forty-five cities in thirty-five days. We made so much money on that tour that the promoters couldn't count all the money. We had to put it in bags and throw it in the back of the bus.

It was a great comeback. Stan was back in the drum chair of a top band with a sponsorship and a shiny new set to boot. "Stan Levey was really glad to have the opportunity to play with the band," said composer, arranger, and baritone saxophonist Gerry Mulligan. "Kenton was very kind and gave him a chance to re-establish himself after having been all the way down, so Stan made a really major effort to please Kenton, musically."

Best of all, he was free from addiction and officially engaged to Angela, who joined the tour as the drummer's bride-to-be.

"After a while, I didn't like how it looked," said Angela. "You know, 'the girl on the bus.' My mother was living in Florida, and Stan wanted to get on her good side by getting married down there once we finally had some time off, which was many months away. I told him I either wanted to get married sooner or stay with my friend in D.C. We were nearby at the Bolling Air Force Base, and the bus driver had already agreed to take me into the city. Stan and I started arguing on the bus in the parking lot after the show. It got louder, and we moved outside in front of these enormous headlights, yelling at each other. Everybody on the bus thought it was hilarious. They were yelling, 'Get married and get back on the bus!'"

Stan and Angela chose Atlantic City for their wedding.

Kenton had a two-week engagement at Steel Pier, and Grandma Hoffman could help with preparations and accommodations.

Grandma Hoffman arranged for the ceremony at the Beth Kehilla Synagogue. Before the wedding, Essie caused Stan to have a small fit when she charmed Kenton's arranger, Gene Rowland, a man Stan did not like. Angela's Sicilian Catholic mother, Adele, refused to attend and remained deeply troubled about her daughter's marriage to a Jewish jailbird.

On July 30, 1952, Stan and Angela exchanged vows. The seats were filled with the entire Kenton organization and other musicians from New Jersey and Philadelphia. Angela wore an off-white dress with robin's-egg-blue shoes and a matching hat with veil. Stan Kenton gave the reception at a guesthouse with expansive grounds. It was a large celebration hindered only by stiflingly hot temperatures. Kenton even provided a de facto honeymoon for the young couple in the form of his upcoming European tour.

Aside from Adele's disapproval, the only thing impeding the newlyweds' marital bliss was a letter from Shirley's lawyer demanding money for Robert's child support.

"Stan went to Kenton and told him he might have to search for a higher-paying job," said Angela. "Kenton asked Stan how much he owed each month and gave Stan that much of a raise. He was such a mensch."

The last thing Stan wanted to do was disappoint his generous boss, but his standing with Kenton was tested in Atlantic City in 1953, when Stan was arrested by the highest drug officer in the land.

Popular culture remembers Harry Anslinger as a bit of a laughingstock for promoting "reefer madness" with racially charged propaganda. Less widely remembered are Anslinger's achievements as a mob-buster. While the FBI under J. Edgar

Hoover was denying the existence of a national crime syndicate, Anslinger's Federal Bureau of Narcotics agents were penetrating the heroin network in Kansas City, investigating the very men who first supplied Charlie Parker. What the agents found radiating from the heart of America was chilling in its breadth, scope, and treachery, and presented for the first time proof of a sinister national organized crime syndicate dominated by Italians.

Documenting the Mafia was an enormous breakthrough, but Anslinger's revelations failed to catch on. The notion of a secret, interconnected ethnic syndicate seemed incredible, and jokes circulated of FBN agents being under the influence of substances taken from their own evidence lockers. It would take J. Edgar Hoover almost two more decades to admit its existence. Meanwhile, Anslinger built cases. The tentacles reaching out from Kansas City led to St. Louis, Chicago, Tampa, New York, Sicily, and Turkey. Anslinger dispatched agents to southern Europe and eastern Asia. He became one of the Mafia's great nemeses, and a bitter enemy of crime kingpin Lucky Luciano, who infuriated Anslinger by manipulating his own release from prison, working with the U.S. Office of Naval Intelligence to protect the New York waterfront and assist with the allied invasion of Sicily. Luciano was released in 1946 and deported to Italy, but he turned up later that year in Cuba, where he was positioning himself for backdoor access to the United States. In what was perhaps his most satisfying victory, Commissioner Anslinger convinced President Harry Truman to pressure the Cuban government by threatening to block all shipments of medical narcotics to the island. The reluctant Cubans sent a furious Luciano back to Italy.

If there was one group of people Anslinger reviled almost as much as mobsters, it was jazz musicians. His agents kept many under surveillance and they arrested, among others, Charlie Parker and Billie Holiday. Anslinger kept an ever-expanding file called "Marijuana and Musicians" and planned for a "great national round-up arrest of musicians in violation of the marijuana laws all on a single day."

"We *will* have a national round-up," Anslinger wrote to his field offices. "Don't worry, I will tell you what day."

In 1948, Anslinger went before a senate committee to request funding for more agents. In response to the senators' questions regarding the type of people who were flaunting the nation's narcotics laws, Anslinger answered, "Musicians."

A pause ensued, and Anslinger continued, "And I don't mean good musicians. I mean jazz musicians!"

Anslinger's superiors at the Treasury Department quashed his national roundup, but the FBN continued to pursue jazz musicians on individual drug cases. Anslinger's personal appearance at Stan's arrest effectively confirmed that Stan had been under surveillance since leaving prison, and it anticipated headlines related to the wildly popular Kenton band—a pretty safe bet, since so few ex-junkies stayed clean.

I was walking into the ballroom at the Steel Pier, carrying my cymbal bag, when I was surrounded by agents. Harry Anslinger, the head of the Federal Bureau of Narcotics, was there. He was the top guy, man, from Washington. I was arrested. They take me to the men's room and I had to urinate in a bottle, which I shouldn't have done because they probably could have done something to it, put something in there. But in those days I figure, "Well, no problem. I'm clean." I guess they wanted to make the headlines. It had all the elements: "Drummer in nation's top band arrested on narcotics charges, just out of prison, making his way back." You know.

He picked the wrong guy.

George Morte, the band manager, came and bailed me out. I had to pay a small fine, even though I hadn't done anything. It had something to do with an obscure Atlantic City statute—not registering as an ex-convict. I was an hour late to the job, but Kenton let the whole thing pass. It's all in the papers the next day. The ACLU contacted me about suing, but I just wanted to be done with it. And that, finally, was the end of it.

With Anslinger off his back, Stan had the good fortune of participating in what was perhaps Kenton's finest year. In 1953, the band conquered Europe and also completed what became Kenton's magnum opus: an extraordinary collaboration with arranger Bob Graettinger called *City of Glass*.

It was unlike anything else in jazz—an adventure into a futuristic soundscape of dreamy, multi-layered dissonance. Even some of Kenton's harshest critics have praised this spellbinding, semi-classical work. Critic John F. Szwed, who found much of what Kenton did "pretentious and tasteless," described the music on *City of Glass* as "luminous, shimmering concert works whose brilliant use of instruments can still shock fifty years later."

Over time, *City of Glass* became a shining star in Kenton's enormous discography. For Stan Levey it represents perhaps his most avant-garde appearance on record. The European tour was a sensation, with jazz-starved fans traveling across national borders to hear the great American band.

"Coming in at the Berlin airport, there were open cars parading the band around like they were politicians," Angela said. "In every city, there were crowds in the streets and big bouquets of flowers in everyone's arms. There were newspaper articles in every different language. The crowds at the concerts were enormous—twenty thousand in Berlin alone. Stan lost about seven pounds each night, with water just pouring off him.

"We were in Amsterdam, Dusseldorf, London, Paris. In Paris, one of my absolute favorite musical things was done —'Zoot.' Oh, I just think it's to die over! I can't stand still when I hear it. Italy was the only place the wives didn't go. We stayed in London. On the train between Germany and Paris, Stan got mad once when Kenton knocked on our compartment door and saw me in my slip. He was usually good about hiding any sort of jealousy, but the tour tested everyone's patience.

"Frank Rosolino was hilarious on that tour. We went around on a very nice bus, and Frank would take over the microphone from Herr Hoffmeister and say things like, 'We're now passing over the Rhine River, and the reason it's called the Rhine is because the riverbed is paved with rhinestones.'

"Stan was always very careful because he knew so many criminals and thugs and was one himself, at one time. But in what I call his *second* life, he always took great precautions. In Essen, Germany, we had our passports in his camera bag between his feet under the table, and it got stolen. We had to go from there into Vienna and had to lie on the floor of the bus because we didn't have passports. The police found it when the thief tried to pawn it, and they gave it to us later.

"Kenton provided for me and five other band wives as well. He was such a gentleman. Quite honestly, Stan Kenton was one of the nicest, most decent, and elegant men you'd want to meet. Just a lovely man."

There was a period when we all used separate cars, about eight or nine, instead of the band bus. My wife and I drove with Stan in his Lincoln, along with Bob Burgess and Ernie Royal. I don't know what godforsaken place we were in—somewhere in Montana or Wyoming—but the road turned and we didn't. So we flew straight up and were actually airborne. It was nothing serious but when we landed, Bobby Burgess was out of the car standing! We couldn't figure out how this happened. He must have got out in midair. It's the quickest move I ever saw in my life.

We go to a motel in a tiny town. It looks like the Bates Motel. The guy behind the desk, he looks at us, three great big guys and Ernie Royal, who's black, with this gorgeous woman [Angela], and says, "Who's the whoremaster here?" Kenton says, "Sir, we just need four rooms and a little less conversation."

I prefer small groups. You can stretch out a bit and make a statement. With a big band, you're limited by the chart. You've got to play the arrangement, and there's only so much you can do with that. There are so many built-in advantages in small bands. They're for flying. Big bands, by comparison, are for walking, and sometimes with difficulty. With a big band, you have to shepherd the herd. Move it around the way it should be moved. It's not easy. Takes a lot of concentration and a lot of devotion to the beat. You've got to keep all the ends tucked in. I always visualize the drummer sitting more or less in the center of a big band, trying to control and unite this bunch of musicians. Some of the players are not easily guided and slip out of your grasp. These are the ones who give me the mental picture of tucking in the ends. If you don't do that, you're going to lose them. They'll just stop. Your job is to make it go forward. You have to be Big

Daddy. You're always trying to whip people into order, while doing your best to establish a good feeling and move the band forward.

It was a tough, physically demanding job for a drummer. I used to break very large Zildjian cymbals regularly. Twenty-two, twenty-four-inch cymbals. That's how loud I was playing at the time. The Zildjian people told me they were happy when I left the band and retired to quieter work. I used to crack 'em pretty good, and it got expensive. It was hard work, you know. Ten brass. That's a lot of work. I wasn't too thrilled with the rhythm section, and that goes for myself, too. I'm sure the other guys were more than adequate, but the section never jelled. Probably the band was too overpowering, you couldn't *move* or maneuver the ensemble too easily.

In 1954, Kenton did something called the Festival of Modern American Jazz, which was the Kenton band touring with featured stars like Dizzy, Charlie Parker, Nat Cole, Erroll Garner, and Sarah Vaughan. There was a bus for the stars and one for the band. One time I was riding with the stars, watching a poker game, and Erroll Garner was winning big. The bus hits a bump, Garner goes up, and there's an ace on his seat!

When Bird first came on with us, somebody had touted him to see Bill Russo, so Bird comes to me and says, "I'm going to get Bill to do my arrangements." I said, "Great, Holman is really into your music." Bird told me he meant Bill Russo and when he said that I told him, "Man, you're going to the wrong Bill! Who you want to see is Bill Holman." Russo was a good arranger, but not of that ilk. He was more like a college professor sometimes, the way Stan would let him make those intellectual speeches in front of the band.

Parker was in dire straits on that tour. He looked awful. Fat, sick, could hardly play. One night, Dizzy tells Bird that Lee Konitz is playing him off the bandstand. From that night on, Bird just somehow reinvents himself. He dug way down in his psyche somewhere and began to play better. Sounded pretty good, let me tell you. But he'd shuffle across the stage like an old man. Terrible pain, heart trouble, lues, terrible ulcers, short of breath. No strength. He did three numbers. That's all he could do.

In Cleveland, I went to the men's room before the show and I hear this groaning like a death rattle from one of the stalls. Someone is dying in there. It gets louder, and I say, "Sir, is there anything I can do?"

"No, Stanley, I'm all right, don't worry. I'll be all right."

It's Bird in there. He's in there for about fifteen minutes, and I wait. He can't eat or drink. I ask him how he's going to play, but he says, "I'll play, I've got to have the money." He looks like a guy near the end of his rope, but he goes out and plays. Terrible pain. Passing blood—just a total mess. That's what happens when you have too much fun. Bird was idolized. He could have had anything he wanted, but he wouldn't behave, so he got nothing. He got jerked around.

We said goodbye at the airport. From me it was meant for later, but he was saying goodbye for good. He was very insightful. He knew.

CHAPTER 9

BIRD LIVES!

While Stan was serving his time in prison, Bird was solidifying his reputation as the most awe-inspiring jazz musician of any instrument. He collected a congregation of imitators, the best of whom became stars in their own right. He was a human turning point whose innovations marked the dawn of a new musical landscape. He was so highly regarded in the jazz world that the hippest club outside of Fifty-Second Street—Birdland—was named after him.

Bird also continued to career from one calamity to another. His erratic behavior sometimes got him banned from the very club that bore his name. Angela Levey, who knew Bird well through both Stan and her job at Birdland, still gets agitated when remembering the man who hooked her husband on heroin.

"Bird," she said. "Yes, well, to be honest with you, he got on my nerves. I did like him—his intelligence, his good sense of humor. But our relationship was contentious. I was just furious with him for obvious reasons, for doing that to Stan.

"We saw him all the time, but I didn't want him playing with my kid, so to speak. I put limits on how much he could play with Stan, and he didn't like that. One time I stopped by a daytime jam session at the Brill Building across from Birdland.

All the Tin Pan Alley songwriters had offices there. Somehow they would get a room there just to jam.

"Bird comes in and says to Stan, 'Billy Strayhorn will be up at Minton's tonight, and we're invited to sit in.'

"'Well,' I said softly, 'Stan can't go.'

"Stan plays along and says, 'Bird . . . she says I can't go, I can't go.'

"Oh, Bird looked like he would blow his top! He *hated* that! Whenever he saw me, he would salute me as if I were a Mafia boss or the chief of police.

"At Birdland, there were lots of stairs that came down to a landing where I was sitting, selling tickets. Just a metal box with money in it. I had to guard it. Bird would come down the steps—he thought he could run everything—and say, 'Angela, please go pay the cab.'

"'What is wrong with you?' I'd say. 'I can't just leave here.' He'd say, 'Will you please go ask Morris or Irving to pay the cab?'

"One time, he brought in the new recording of *Charlie Parker with Strings* for Irv and Morris to listen to. There was a back room sort of an office, and I went in there and I heard a little of it and then I left to go back to work. Later, Bird comes out, very perturbed, and says, 'You could've given it more than one minute!'

"It was that way between us right up to the last time I laid eyes on him. One time at Birdland, Stan was playing with Kenton right before we went to Europe. I was sitting in the booth near the bandstand door, next to the kitchen. Stan was onstage and Bird came and sat with me. We talked and laughed a little, and then Stan joined us at intermission and Bird says to Stan, 'You know . . . you still owe me seventy dollars.'

"'How dare you!' I shout. 'You owe him your life!'

"He got up and walked straight into the kitchen, and I went in after him. He went out the other side, and I just kept following him, yelling at him the whole way."

As Dizzy—ever the shrewd businessman—prospered, Parker imprisoned himself in debt, a slave to his addiction. The seventy dollars Stan owed Bird was good for little beyond his next few fixes. One jazz anecdote has Bird showing his needle marks to a friend, saying, "This is my Cadillac," then lifting his other arm and lamenting, "This is my house." In a bitter irony, the *artiste* who abhorred gratuitous amusement ended up, as Ralph Ellison said, as "entertainment for a ravenous, sensation-starved, culturally disoriented public . . . like a man dismembering himself with a dull razor on a spotlighted stage." Louis Armstrong may have goofed and grinned onstage, but he never pissed himself in public.

Charlie Parker died at the age of thirty-four on March 12, 1955, in the apartment of British baroness Pannonica de Koenigswarter, a wealthy jazz patron connected to the Rothschild family. His body was so ravaged that the coroner estimated his age to be fifty-three.

Word spread in the newspapers of the tragic Negro genius who died in a baroness's apartment. The spray-painted slogan "Bird Lives!" appeared on brick walls in Greenwich Village. Eulogies offered by fellow musicians bestowed on Bird the status of an immediate legend. "He could sue almost everybody who's made a record in the last ten years," said Lennie Tristano. Cootie Williams called Bird "the greatest individual musician who ever lived," and went on to say, ". . . every instrument in the band tried to copy Charlie Parker, and in the history of jazz there had never been one man who influenced all the instruments."

Even now, Parker is rarely spoken of without similar strings of superlatives to describe his stratospheric talent and singular influence on modern music. Three quarters of a century after his death, Charlie Parker is still the Bird fluttering high above the heads of mere mortal musicians. In 2013, jazz critic Dan Morgenstern said, "Parker's ability to create meaningful, even beautiful, music at tempos hitherto unknown—he was a speed demon—has not been equaled to this day. Yes, there are players who can execute at such tempos, but not with musical and emotional content."

Every year on August 29, musicians like alto saxophonist Bobby Watson gather around Parker's gravesite in Kansas City for a moving ceremony that turns raucous with the annual "Twenty-One Saxophone Salute." Such tributes, almost a hundred years after his birth and sixty years after his death, attest to a reverence reserved for the very few.

In the annals of jazz history, Stan Levey is invariably linked to Charlie Parker as a fellow bebop pioneer, as the drummer who was with Bird and Diz at the very beginning and when they introduced bop to the West Coast on the storied California excursion. But Stan missed the Guild session as he toured with Woody Herman, and Bird missed the Dial session in California, so Stan's recorded output with Bird is tiny in proportion to the amount they actually played together. As Bird's roommate and go-to guy for jam sessions, Stan's major contributions to Parker's music are lost in unrecorded improvisations that no doubt make up some of the most compelling music the saxophonist ever played. The lack of recorded material has resulted in Stan Levey generally receiving short shrift in the legion of Parker biographies, a fact which led the drummer to take a bit of jovial pride in his own personal piece of Parker trivia, something only he could claim: Bird, who was infamous for borrowing, stealing, and owing *everyone* money, died before collecting Stan's seventy dollars, making Stan the only cat in history who owed Charlie Parker money.

CHAPTER 10

WEST COAST COOL

S tan's old roommate, Miles Davis, is widely credited with launching cool jazz. It was the first giant step the master innovator took on his trailblazing career path. Sessions recorded in 1948 and '49 resulted in the album *Birth of the Cool*.

Staking claim to an entire movement was something the record company did on Miles's behalf, but few were arguing. Miles himself claimed it almost casually. After all, it was the impression of effortlessness that made cool jazz cool.

Miles's relative modesty on the subject was also an acknowledgement of the other musicians on the project: an interracial collective that Davis co-led with arranger Gil Evans and baritone saxophonist Gerry Mulligan. Lee Konitz, Stan's future bandmate in Kenton's outfit, was a featured soloist, along with J. J. Johnson on trombone. The unusual instrumentation of the nine-piece band utilized French horn, baritone sax, and tuba to color African American music with impressionistic elements of European harmony.

The racial cooperation was as fresh as the music. Unlike the random infusion of a few white musicians like Stan Levey into the thoroughly Negro art form of bebop, this was a more purposeful collaboration of traditions, with some of the finest young black and white musicians coming together to create something new and achingly beautiful. "We all influenced each other, and Bird influenced us all," said Gerry Mulligan.

According to Miles, the experiment also created tensions.

"A lot of black musicians came down on my case about their not having work, and here I was hiring white guys in my band," he said. "So I just told them if a guy could play as good as Lee Konitz played, I would hire them every time."

By Miles's own admission, the band was emulating the suspended-in-the-air sounds of the Claude Thornhill Orchestra, a white band playing Gil Evans arrangements. But Miles was quick to point out that Thornhill's sound grew out of Duke Ellington, so what was white before it was black was actually black before it was white.

The layers of color and implied tension made for marvelous music. Cool jazz smoothed out and sweetened the jarring elements of bop and added counterpoint to the mix. Subdued rhythms and a seamless flow from written to improvised passages made listeners feel relaxed yet alert. A revived emphasis on composition was balanced with openness to experimentation.

Cool jazz arrived just in time for the 1950s, and rose contemporaneously with the huge postwar population shift to the West Coast. Many white musicians moved to Los Angeles, where club work and record dates could be supplemented with studio soundtrack work for movies and television. The studios hired black musicians, but white musicians generally had an easier time landing the good-paying jobs. A collection of white talent steeped in the cool school—Gerry Mulligan chief among them—clustered around Los Angeles. Like previous assemblages of jazz talent in New Orleans, Kansas City, and Manhattan, it was another organic grouping of creative minds and diverse tone colors. Cool jazz evolved into "West Coast jazz" and the sound began to reflect the laid-back atmosphere of the sun and surf in the Golden State. Stan Levey, who had brought bebop to California with Bird and Diz a few years earlier, now became instrumental in the development of West Coast jazz. He and another East Coast transplant, Shelly Manne, became the first-call drummers in California.

"Stan and Shelly were good friends," said Angela. "He was married to Flip, and we knew them very well. They always had horses. Shelly was not at all a rival to Stan. There was never any of that. Even when Shelly had more work, Stan never felt that way. [It was] one thing Stan was very adamant about. He'd always say, 'Nobody *owes* me a job.' He really believed that."

Working alongside Stan and Shelly Manne was a key group of Kenton alumni and a revolving cast of all-stars who played in the house band at the famous Lighthouse Club in Hermosa Beach.

I was with Kenton—what—three years? We finished out the big festival with Nat Cole and Dizzy and Sarah in Los Angeles. We played our last date and the band was going to break up for a couple of weeks. I went to LAX to fly home, and they're yelling my name over the big speaker: "Paging Stan Levey! Phone call, sir!"

I'm thinking, "What happened? What did I do?" So I go to the red phone and it's my old friend Max Roach calling.

"Stan!"

"Yeah Max, what's going on?"

"Look, I'm working at the Lighthouse at Hermosa Beach. You've got to get me out of here. I have a six-month contract and I can't get out unless I get a suitable replacement. You're the guy. They'll settle on you."

The "suitable replacement" clause in Max's Lighthouse

contract was the work of Howard Rumsey, an older Kenton bassist who created and led the All-Stars for the Lighthouse's owner, John Levine. It was one of the ways Rumsey ensured top-shelf jazz five nights a week, fifty-two weeks a year. Roach was eager to break away and start his own band with Clifford Brown. Since there were only a few drummers in the whole country considered comparable, he was in a bind.

I went right from the airport to the Lighthouse, talked to Max and Howard Rumsey and John Levine and we settled on a price and I took the job. Two hundred a week. The very next day, Max was gone and I started. That was the beginning of a good, long relationship with Howard and the Lighthouse.

The Lighthouse was right on the beach—30 Pier Avenue. The doors were wide open. People wore Hawaiian shirts and came in and out and back and forth to the beach, dripping sand and sweat, you know. A great young crowd, and they loved the music. It was a fantastic atmosphere. It cost nothing to go to the Lighthouse. You walked in, sat down, had a drink, maybe dinner. The food was good. Everybody sat in. Miles, Dizzy, Dexter. Pick a name, they've been there.

For Stan, it was a golden opportunity to settle in California with a steady job, plus side work in the studios. It all sounded wonderful to Angela, who flew out from her mother's in D.C. with little more than one suitcase.

The happy couple found a furnished apartment in Hermosa Beach. Angela became fast friends with Howard Rumsey's wife, Joyce, and the All-Stars and their wives took to having a bite to eat together after the show. Angela perfected her coconut cake and improved their furnishings. She also trained her

Stan and Essie at the beach in Atlantic City, circa 1930.

Young Stan in Atlantic City, circa 1937.

i

Stan jamming on Ellis Tollin's drums at the Spotlite with Leonard Gaskin and Charlie Parker, 1945.

Stan, Leonard Gaskin, Charlie Parker, Miles Davis, and Dexter Gordon playing at the Spotlite, 1945.

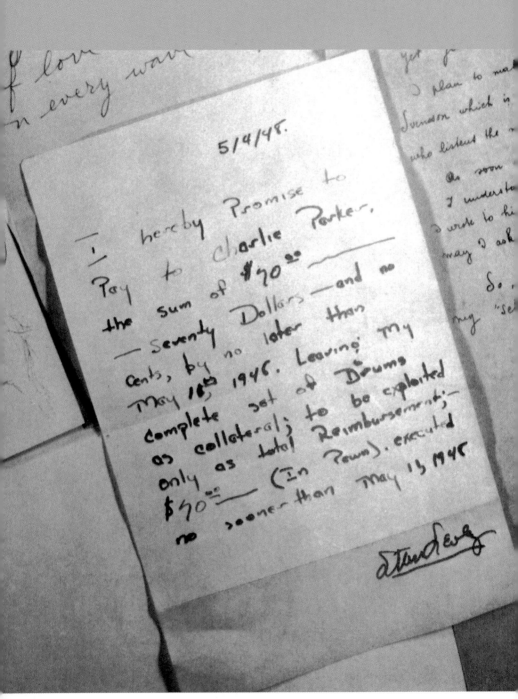

Stan's IOU to Charlie Parker, 1948.

Above: Curly Russell, Allen Eager, George Wallington, and Stan playing at the Three Deuces, 1948.

Below: Joan Kamuca, Richie Kamuca, Jonie Kamuca, Stan, Angela, and Frank Rosolino at the Rustic Cabin in New Jersey, circa 1952.

Angela and Stan at the Casino Royale in Washington D.C., circa 1952.

Stan with
one of his
early Ludwig
kits, 1952.

stars
surround
Stan...

*Stan Levey is a man whose career is shaped by stars. Not the astrological variety, however. Stan's affairs are influenced by such stars as Frank Sinatra, Peggy Lee, Nelson Riddle, and Billy May—to name just a few.

It was because of requests from luminaries of this magnitude that Stan recently left a successful, longtime gig at the Lighthouse, in Los Angeles, and is concentrating on recording dates.

Stan appears on a vast majority of Verve albums, sitting in with such diverse talents as Gerry Mulligan, Oscar Peterson, Diz Gillespie, Stan Getz, Ben Webster and Jimmy Guiffre.

He's also to be heard on Contemporary, Dot, RCA Victor, Mode, Bethlehem and United Artists issues.

A star's star—that's Stan. And whenever you hear Levey, you hear LUDWIGS... most famous name on drums!

Heard about Ludwig's new
Super-Sensitive Snare Drum?
It whispers or thunders with a tonal vividness and response you'll call miraculous! Each individual snare strand is attached to its own tension screw. A dual throw-off releases the snares from both sides at once. A second set of gut snares can be mounted in less than a minute! Hear it soon! You'll agree—this is the FINEST snare drum ever designed!

HERE'S THE *Ludwig* COMBINATION
THAT STAN LEVEY PREFERS

Ludwig   MOST FAMOUS
NAME
ON DRUMS

Stan enjoyed a long relationship
with Ludwig drums, 1952.

Stan playing the piano, 1952.

Publicity shot taken just after Stan joined the Stan Kenton Orchestra, 1952.

Above: Ernie Royal accompanying Stan on tambourine with the Stan Kenton Orchestra, early 1950s.

Below: Publicity shot of Stan, 1953.

Above: Stan Kenton with band members (*clockwise from bottom*) June Christy, Frank Rosolino, Zoot Sims, and Don Dennis, early 1950s.

Below: Stan Kenton and his star singer, June Christy, with a tour poster, 1953.

Above: Stan Kenton studying arrangements, circa 1953.

Below: Lorraine Gillespie, Dizzy Gillespie, unknown, June Christy, Stan, and unknown.

Charlie Parker, Bill Russo, Barry Galbraith, Stan, and Don Bagley playing Stan Kenton's Festival of Modern American Jazz at the Shrine Auditorium, 1954.
©Ross Burdick/ CTSIMAGES

Stan took this photograph of Charlie Parker in 1954, just before the saxophonist departed from Stan Kenton's tour. It was the last time he ever saw Bird.

Above: Stan had top billing at the Lighthouse, 1955.

Below: Stan, Bud Shank, Jack Sheldon, Bob Cooper, and Howard Rumsey playing at the Lighthouse, 1955.

Opposite: Stan playing a solo at the Lighthouse, mid-1950s.

In the 1950s, Stan taught boxing
fundamentals to pianist Vince Guaraldi,
who took these training photos of Stan.

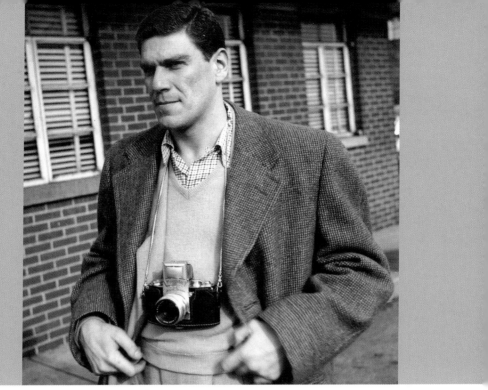

Above: Stan with one of his first cameras, mid-1950s.
Below: Stan Getz, taken by Stan, mid-1950s.

Above: Angela and Stan in Hermosa Beach, 1955.

Below: Stan rehearsing with Dexter Gordon, Conte Candoli, and Frank Rosolino, 1955.

Opposite: Big man, small kit, mid-1950s.

Stan with his hero and teacher,
Dizzy Gillespie, 1956.

Dizzy Gillespie playing
with Stan's son, Chris,
while visiting the Levey
home in Hermosa Beach,
circa 1956.

Lighthouse All-Stars Frank Rosolino, Stan, Bob Cooper, Howard Rumsey, and Victor Feldman, 1957.

Above: Max Roach and Stan Levey on the set for *Drummin' the Blues*, 1957.

Below: Publicity photo of Shelly Manne taken by Stan, late 1950s.

Above: Publicity photo of Sonny Clark taken by Stan, late 1950s.

Below: Frank Rosolino and Stan at the back door of the Lighthouse, circa 1958.

Stan took this album cover photo for his friend, Lou Levy, in 1959. The "band" is Chris Levey on clarinet, David Levey on drums, and Lou's daughter, Diane Levy, on trumpet.

Stan's three sons, (*left to right*) Chris, Robert, and David, circa 1964.

One of Stan's first jobs as a photographer was this shoot with Buddy Rich and his trumpet section for a Martin Band Instrument Company advertisement, mid-1960s.

Above: From drummer to percussionist, mid-1960s.

Below: Stan working a television soundtrack session, early 1970s.

STAN LEVEY

A. 13″ Hi-Hats (New Beat)
B. 15″ Fast-Crash (Medium)
C. 18″ Ride (Medium)

Stan in the twilight of his music career, early 1970s.

Angela and Stan in Hawaii, 1970s.

Above: Lalo Schifrin and Stan, 2003.

Below: Stan with Quincy Jones, his old friend from Fifty-Second Street, 2003.

Opposite: Stan in 2003.

Stan with Rolling Stones drummer Charlie Watts, 2003.

husband to save and invest money, a virtue he embraced. Soon they had their first car, a Chrysler woodie.

Robert Levey remembered meeting his father very clearly. "My mother told me one day, 'You're going to meet your father,'" he said.

"We pulled up and there he was, standing there in a yellow sweater," said Angela. "He was five or six years old."

"Here was this big, stoic guy," Robert said. "He was intimidating. No hugs or anything like that. He took me around . . . we did a lot of things. That was it for a while. But I used to go stay with them at Hermosa Beach in the summer. There was a stand on Pier Avenue that sold coconut and pineapple juice, and I'd drink about ten of those a day. Angela would've had a fit if she knew. Later on, I'd go into the Lighthouse and watch the old man. He was a piece of energy. The sweat! Working like a machine. Intense."

"The things Stan heard from Robert were atrocious," said Angela. "One time when Robert was over, the news was on. I knew instantly . . . it was his mother being taken out on a stretcher. She'd tried to commit suicide. In one split second I grabbed him and said, 'Bath time!'

"She left a note, and the tabloids got a hold of it. She was that type . . . knew how to get her name around. She wasn't famous, but she did a few films. In the note, she blamed three men: Frank Sinatra, Jerry Lewis, and Stan Levey. Stan was *so* embarrassed.

"I would pick Robert up as often as I could. When he got older, it became harder."

Stan's journey from ex-con to family man was complete in 1955, when his son, Christopher, was born. By the time Angela was pregnant with their second son, David, they had bought a house on La Tijera Street.

"In November, it got a little cold," remembered Angela. "We went to look for the heater and there wasn't one."

Stan's job provided the security he needed to support his growing family, but it was hard work. "Cool" generally stopped at the Lighthouse door. The All-Stars served up stomping swing, burning bebop, and spicy Latin numbers. Aggressive jam sessions kept the scene hopping, and Stan was frequently called on to solo.

> We had a full plate five nights a week, and studio work in the daytime and off-site concerts and stuff, so we were busy. Sunday was a full twelve-hour concert: 2:00 PM to 2:00 AM. Whew! Right around the clock.

At the Lighthouse, Stan proved he was as reliable as he was musical. Howard Rumsey called him "Mr. Consistency" because he never missed a performance. One of Stan's loyal fans at the Lighthouse, Hoagy Charmichael Jr., wrote this remembrance: "The sounds of Lighthouse jazz gave me, as a teenager, a window into a new world of experimental music and free expression. I can still see Stan up on that stand, the earnest provider of time, hands flying and feet moving confidently down the middle of the groove. The sound of his crisp high hat, and the light dancing off the accents of his black pearl kit, all not six feet from me. His occasional nod from that Hermosa pier bandstand as I sat just under him gave me a lifeline to some of the greatest music this country has spawned."

West Coast jazz soon met its match with hard bop, a self-consciously black sound that answered the emotional reserve of cool by simplifying the complex chord changes of bebop and infusing them with churchy, blues-drenched call-and-response harmonies that welcomed early elements of soul and funk into the mix.

The tension between West Coast and hard bop created something not unlike the hype of a heavyweight match between white and black fighters. Industry executives understood the allure of competition between the races, and the notion of a black thing in the East versus a white thing out West didn't hurt record sales. Two distinct jazz styles were hip at the same time and competition between the two, whether real or manufactured, helped elevate both into highly refined and inspired art forms. With its richness and diversity, jazz in the 1950s reached its high water mark in popularity and sales.

But the racial divide was more illusion than reality. Jazz remained interracial on both coasts, and the musicians continued to cross back and forth over the social, geographic, and musical boundaries. Stan Levey would become the quintessential white cat on the coast while continuing to work closely with many of the best black artists in the business.

Howard always picked the best that he could get. It was an experimental place. He was very innovative when it came to finding new players. It was kind of a drummer's showcase: Shelly, Max, then me. And he would have good composers. Let the guys in the band do what they could do. If you wrote something, they'd play it, and if it sounded good it would go into the book. He was wide open. Howard's a good guy. Provided a lot of work for a lot of people. Good money it paid me. Fifty-two weeks a year. Great security.

How do I say this nicely? Howard was not a good player. He knew it. It wasn't like he didn't know it. I could only carry him so long.

But I want to make one statement about Howard. The kind of guy he is. To this day, when I talk to him—it's amazing.

He says, "Stan, I've got to apologize. The way I played was just—how did you put up with it?"

And I say to him, "Howard, every guy on that bandstand never gave less than the best they could give, every night." And that's the truth. He never laid down, and we didn't either. "No, man. You created a lot of work for a lot of people." Good guy. *Really* good guy.

We had Mondays and Tuesdays off. On those days, different little groups like Jimmy Giuffre would come in. Harold Land subbed for Bob Cooper when he left for Europe. Frank Butler was sitting in, scaring everybody on drums. Sometimes I was afraid to listen. Don Cherry and Ornette Coleman—I call him "Ornate" Coleman—they played there. Didn't get it. Don't get it. No structure, no chords. Two chord, one chord? Maybe no chord? Going nowhere? I mean, what the hell's that? Charlie Haden I know real well. Played with him. Outstanding player. But Coleman, for me, was more like sound effects than music.

The Lighthouse gig allowed us to stay in town and do a lot of studio work and record dates. A lot of people from the Hollywood studios started coming down: James Coburn, Lee Marvin, Marlon Brando, the Smothers Brothers, Liberace. We all worked in the studios, too, and Howard—if we had a nighttime recording—he'd let us off, as long as you'd get a good sub. A lot of us came from the Kenton thing, so we had camaraderie. I was involved with so many great players on that bandstand: Victor Feldman, Sonny Clark, Conte Candoli, Frank Rosolino, Bud Shank, Marty Paich. Tremendous players.

Of all the tremendous players, Conte Candoli and Frank Rosolino shared the closest musical association with Stan.

Stan's involvement with Candoli went back to Woody Herman and continued through Kenton, the Lighthouse, and dozens of record dates. The boisterous trumpeter played on every one of Stan's own albums, and Candoli's blistering improvisations were just the thing for the jam sessions at the Lighthouse.

Frank Rosolino was born to Sicilian immigrants in the fertile jazz city of Detroit. Mischievous and hilarious, Rosolino was one of the most beloved cats in the business. Frank's friends, frequently exhausted from sidesplitting laughter—had to beg him to stop being funny. Gene Lees, who sketched the seminal literary portrait of Frank in his book *Meet Me at Jim and Andy's*, wrote, "I don't think any man ever had more friends or fewer enemies than Frank Rosolino . . . One of the finest trombone players in the history of the instrument, he had a superb tone, astonishing facility, a deep Italianate lyricism, and rich invention. Frank was, very simply, a sensational player."

"Frank's wife, Jean, and I were best friends," said Angela. "Very good together . . . very close. Stan and I traveled with them . . . she told me that sometimes Frank was very moody and I just couldn't believe it with that big grin on his face with the mustache. At their house in Garden Grove, they gave me a baby shower and there must have been a hundred people there. His playing, I mean . . . my God, I haven't heard anything like it before or since. Marvelous! Neither Frank nor Conte were very deep intellectually, as far as I could tell. I guess that doesn't have anything to do with being a genius musically."

But of all the cats on the Lighthouse scene, Stan Levey was the only one who was a bona-fide bebop pioneer. His reputation preceded him and added to his intimidating image. Jim Keltner, the "Wrecking Crew" drummer who frequented the

Lighthouse as a teenager before recording with Bob Dylan and the Rolling Stones, commented on Stan's aura at the time.

"When I was very young, when I first saw him play, he intimidated me," Keltner said. "I thought that he was kind of a scary guy and I would never have wanted to go up and talk to him like I would Mel Lewis or Hal Blaine, or even Shelly. There was something about Stan that was dangerous."

"I got to know Stan quite well during the last three years of his stint at the Lighthouse," said jazz journalist Steven Cerra, "and I came to understand that he had a chip on his shoulder about being self-taught. Young drummers bugged him; they were always asking him technical questions about the instrument. And because he couldn't explain his answers in terminology or 'drum speak,' he usually mumbled something and walked toward the back of the club. What were you going to do, chase after him? The man was huge. He blocked out the sun."

As intimidating as he was physically, Stan's playing was inviting—even nurturing—to the scores of musicians who hired him for their record dates in the 1950s. Quitting Kenton had allowed the cymbal-cracking slugger to recapture and refine his natural style of sophisticated simplicity. Stan's unselfish drumming emphasized support and was often blatantly quiet. It was a tasteful contrast, this powerful drive rendered at low volume, and the biggest guy in the room was never in the way.

"The thing that stands out most when I think of Stan Levey is this really articulate, beautiful, airy sound with the time just *right* up here in your chin," Keltner said. "Just beautiful. No fooling around, not a lot of chitter-chatter . . . but his conversation with the left hand was very articulate and very purposeful. The other thing I remember was the pretty way he'd drop bombs on the bass drum. I always loved that."

The All-Stars recorded frequently and packed in the crowds, including the first generation of surfers. In October of 1954, Dick Williams, the entertainment editor for the *Los Angeles Mirror*, reported that four hundred people were turned away on a Saturday night. Williams also commented on the "uncommonly high percentage of classy, good-looking girls."

But for Stan, there was only Angela. The drummer's wife had nothing to fear from the college co-eds clustered around the bandstand.

"I knew I didn't have to worry, and so did he," said Angela. "One Sunday, I went to June Christy's when Coop [Bob Cooper, Christy's husband and Stan's bandmate] and Stan were working all day and night to see her new baby Shea, and to get all her maternity clothes. Pete Rugolo called and asked us to a party he was having. He said we should come with the baby. We put her in the basket and went. I met Marlon Brando as soon as we came in, and later when I passed Pete on the stairs he said something like, 'Boy, Marlon really likes you.' I immediately went to the phone to call Stan at the Lighthouse and told him. 'Guess who's after me?' Stan said, 'Oh . . . he has good taste. Tell him no checks.' I could've slapped him, but it was funny precisely because the idea of cheating was unthinkable to both of us."

Providing for his wife and family became Stan's passion, and he crammed his hours away from the Lighthouse with record dates and film studio jobs. When their boys were still young, Stan moved his family to North Hollywood to be closer to studio work and a circle of friends whom they enjoyed socializing with. "We didn't like drinking," said Angela. "When we went out, I'd choke one down somehow . . . Stan would have a beer but wouldn't really drink it."

Stan also quit smoking cigarettes. One day, while driving on a freeway in Los Angeles, he heard the news that the surgeon general had officially determined that smoking was dangerous to a person's health. Stan threw his pack out the window and never smoked again. The next day, he refused an audition for *The Steve Allen Show*—the precursor to *The Tonight Show*—because he was crawling with jitters he hadn't experienced since kicking heroin in prison. "That could've been a ten-year gig," Stan joked. "Quitting smoking cost me a couple of million dollars."

Before the boys started junior high, the Leveys moved again to Sherman Oaks, where the family would live for the next forty years. "Every time we moved, he had to check in with the local police as a felon," remembered David Levey. "And he never could vote."

In about—what—1958, I started my photography business. One of my first jobs was to shoot Buddy Rich and his trumpet section for the [Martin Band Instrument Company]. Up to that point, we didn't like each other. I knew him since about '46. He's very sarcastic. He says, "All you photographers are faggots. What do you do? Fashion?"

Somehow we get to be good friends. Around that time, he brings his band into a big place on Santa Monica Boulevard. Every star in town is there: Gregory Peck, Ava Gardner, Rock Hudson, Marilyn Monroe . . . He does the first set: a killer arrangement of the "West Side Story Medley," and they're playing the pants off it. It's like machine guns. His band is steaming. He's a monster up there.

They finish the set, and Buddy's soaked with perspiration. All the stars are ready to be introduced. Buddy goes to the mike and says, "I see all these stars here tonight, but I want to introduce one of the biggest stars of them all. There he is over there . . . ladies and gentlemen . . . Mr. Stan Levey!"

Everybody's like, "*Who?*" They put the spotlight on me, and I'm looking for the nearest table to crawl under. He walks right offstage without introducing anyone else. That's Buddy's sense of humor. I go backstage after the show and Buddy just says, "Hey baby, I introduced you."

One of the last concerts I played with the Lighthouse band was when Gene Norman featured us at the Pasadena Civic Center with several other groups, including Duke Ellington. At the end of the show was a battle of the drummers: Buddy Rich, Gene Krupa, Max Roach, and me, Stan Levey.

I must tell you that Gene Krupa, Max Roach, and Stan Levey all sounded like babies in diapers after Buddy Rich got through with us. It was a wipe-out! There wasn't much we could do about it. We applauded him. He was the most tremendous player. He was surreal. He wasn't real. Just in-human, the things that he did. He was really, really rough on his guys. He'd rip into them, but he was God's gift to the drums.

Later, the Beach Boys and rock-oriented surf music replaced West Coast jazz as the definitive sound of Southern California. Hard bop became the paradigm of modern jazz and the default music at clubs and on jazz radio. White audiences seeking authenticity preferred their jazz as black as possible, and hard bop was easier for ears raised on rock and roll to relate to.

All of this leaves West Coast jazz ripe for rediscovery. Beyond Dave Brubeck and Stan Getz is an inexhaustible collection of music crackling with ideas, virtuosity, and "good vibrations."

CHAPTER 11

THE BIG TIME

The phone rings at my house in North Hollywood. I pick it up. The guy says, "Hello, Stan, it's Benny."

"Benny? Benny who?"

"Benny Goodman."

"Okay, what's the gag?"

"It's me, Stan, Benny Goodman. We're coming out to play Disneyland. I want you in the band."

Now, in his mind, not a second has passed between the last time I saw him when I was sixteen years old. And never mind that he never even spoke to me then. That's the mentality he had. Not, "How are you doing? Are you dead? Are you alive?" Just, "You're going to be in the band."

But I took the job and we played two weeks at Disneyland and there I was, twenty years later, playing with Benny Goodman again. He hadn't changed. Some of his players told me about recording equipment hidden under the stage. He was secretly recording our shows. Somebody called the union and a representative was talking to Benny about it. Later he sent me an album of the stuff he recorded. On the cover he wrote, "To Stan, from Benny—it was a ball!"

One of Benny Goodman's professional achievements had been discovering Peggy Lee, a Swedish-American singer from

North Dakota who joined his orchestra in 1941 and stayed until shortly before young Stan played with the band in Philadelphia. Her star continued to rise, and by the early 1960s she had a collection of top ten hits and international adoration. When she found herself needing a new drummer, her bassist, Max Bennett, who later played with Frank Zappa and Joni Mitchell, recommended Stan.

"Stan and I met at a jam session in Chicago when he was with Kenton," said Bennett. "He had this really great time and could play fast tempos *forever.* He was a boxer, a big guy with a lot of stamina, and in those days in jazz a lot of guys liked to play really up-tempo stuff. And he could sit there and do it twenty-four hours a day. He had this really weird setup. Let's see . . . left-handed, with the sock cymbal on the other side . . . really weird. I'd never seen anybody play like that. By far, one of the best drummers in L.A. We played on a bunch of Bethlehem dates, and then I recommend him to Peggy and he joined the band with Lou Levy and me."

Joining Peggy Lee meant going back on the road, but it was a different kind of road. Two or three weeks in Vegas, two or three more in Tahoe, that kind of thing. Good money. The money was way up there. She didn't work all the time, so I'd do record dates back here. I did about two years with Peggy. We rehearsed from scratch, kind of made up all the arrangements as we went along. When we went to Vegas, New York, Europe, wherever, no one took any music. We knew the stuff cold.

Big-boned, workhorse construction. Three or four packs a day. Drank Courvoisier by the water glass. On the half-break, her hairdresser has that for her and she downs it. After the show it's party time. Goes to bed about 10:00 AM.

She was very ethereal. She could be a little vindictive, but she had a good sense of humor, and she was the consummate artist. One time, she imitated Nat Cole perfectly while he was in the audience. He cried, he was so touched. He loved her. Everyone did. And I really enjoyed working with her.

We had a bongo player. Argentinean guy. Somehow she got tied up with this guy and she married him. I did her wedding pictures as a gift. She comes out of her dressing room with eyes the size of saucers. "What am I doing?" she said. I said, "Peggy, if you're not sure, it's not too late to send him home."

She said, "No, I can't do that."

It lasted a couple of months and she threw him out. She was lonely.

One of the most commercially popular songs Stan played on was Peggy Lee's "I'm a Woman." Along with "Fever," it became her signature song, and was later used to market perfume.

"One time we went to New York," said Max Bennett, "and Stan couldn't go because of that shitty law they had for a long time with the cabaret cards. You had to have a cabaret card to play anyplace that served alcohol, and if you'd been convicted of a felony, you couldn't get one. They relaxed it later, but this time it came up and he couldn't go, so Mel Lewis took Stan's place—or, let's put it this way, he *thought* he did. If you didn't know how good a drummer Mel Lewis was, just ask him. Talk about ego. He was lazy, after playing with Stan Levey, who really played up top, you know? Mel Lewis was a good big band drummer, but I'm sorry, in a trio he was deaf."

Fortunately for Stan, the cabaret card issue didn't come up when Peggy played her most celebrated engagement, four weeks at Basin Street East in Manhattan, where she would reclaim her jazz bona fides before falling back on pop for the rest of her career.

"I remember when I worked with Peggy Lee as the arranger/conductor at Basin Street East," said Quincy Jones. "Opening night was amazing. Ray Charles was there, Count Basie . . . Cary Grant. We had this fantastic rhythm section of Max Bennett, Stan Levey, and Lou Levy."

Many years later, Capitol Records released an album called *Basin Street East Proudly Presents Miss Peggy Lee*. On "Fever," Stan drops delicate bass drum bombs and finger taps an evocative snare behind Peggy's sultry teasing. It's a potent allure, and a perfect example of Peggy's appeal. On "I Love Being Here with You," Peggy tips her hat to Ella Fitzgerald, who was in the audience. Six years earlier, Peggy and Ella had starred together in a movie, *Pete Kelly's Blues*, about a jazz musician at war with Kansas City gangsters. But Peggy and Ella had something else in common: their taste in drummers. On that cold winter night when Peggy turned up the heat at Basin Street East, Ella liked what she heard from that cat Stan, who had once backed her in Philadelphia with his house band.

In truth, Stan didn't much care for the music he was playing every night with Peggy Lee, but he wasn't complaining. For him, musical inspiration and adventure had taken a backseat to making a living and providing for his family.

"Dad took his work very seriously," said David Levey. "He thought of his music as a business, and he treated it that way. I never saw him practice the drums, but later, when he was learning the mallet instruments, he practiced constantly. He called it woodshedding."

When Stan wasn't woodshedding, he was working hard on something else—his fledgling photography business, chores around the house, or arguing with the bank about how much interest they paid. "Since he didn't have a 'real' job, he was a wreck about taking care of his family," said Angela. "He was always scrambling, always hustling."

With his own family flourishing, Stan cautiously allowed Angela to foster a relationship with his mother, who had moved to California with a job at Saks Fifth Avenue and an apartment in Beverly Hills.

"I get a call, three o'clock in the morning," said Stan. "'We have your mother in jail. Common drunk.' *Oy vey.* Here we go again!"

Eventually, though, Essie remarried, moved to Long Beach, and eased up on the liquor. "She was so good with the boys," said Angela. "She was so crazy about them. Stan reluctantly came around."

Essie and her husband, Nat, had a swimming pool where the boys learned to dive underwater by fetching coins that Essie tossed. But Nat didn't live long, and Essie's drinking increased after his death. Stan's resentment hadn't vanished but it had tempered, and his time with his mother on the West Coast had at least a few moments reminiscent of their summer days in Atlantic City.

Stan also made peace with Angela's mother. Adele had come to love her son-in-law, in part because Stan had allowed Angela to raise the boys Catholic. Angela's mother was a regular presence, and the Levey boys enjoyed the benefits of a traditional Italian grandmother. "She'd be standing around the kitchen, guarding the steaming cauldron on the stove, making her signature meatballs for two days," remembered David.

"My mother adored Stan," said Angela. "'What you see is what you get,' she'd say. He just catered to her and treated her great. She knew exactly how to press some of my buttons and if I started arguing with her, Stan would walk up behind her, look at me, and run his finger across his throat like, *Stop.*"

Stan's mother died of liver cancer in 1963. "She got sick and was in the hospital," said Angela. "Stan went to the hospital every single day for at least three weeks." When Stan went through Essie's things after she died, he found albums he had sent her which she had inscribed to herself: "To my loving mother, from Stan."

Essie was buried at Forest Lawn Cemetery in Los Angeles. The son who had surprised her by playing with the King of Swing now considered such work to be routine. She would not have been surprised by his brush with the King of Rock and Roll, either.

One time I was in between shows with Peggy at the Riviera in Las Vegas. I'm playing the slots, and I look over and I see these four guys that look like buildings. And they're looking right at me. Then I see two of them come walking right towards me and I'm getting a little bit nervous. Who are these guys? Gangsters? Union guys? Cops? These two buildings lean in on me and one of them says,

"Elvis Presley."

The guy motions with his thumb, and there he is . . . Elvis Presley.

"He liked the way you played the drums."

Stan's foray into the big time also included playing for John F. Kennedy. Stan came into the Kennedy scene early in the young senator's campaign for the presidency. Campaign rallies were simply paying gigs for Stan, but he admired Kennedy and his acquaintance with the thirty-fifth president became a lifelong source of pride that Angela always knew would bring a smile to his face when the subject arose.

"Tony Curtis and Janet Leigh hosted a campaign rally for Jack Kennedy at the Del Coronado Hotel across the bay from San Diego," said Angela. "Nelson Riddle was playing, and Stan was in the band. I was backstage, standing there listening and looking through a crack in the curtains. I heard a voice say, 'I wonder if they're ready for me yet.'

"He looked nervous. He was buttoning and unbuttoning his coat. His blue shirt matched his blue eyes and his bronze skin matched his bronze hair. I said, 'I don't know, they look pretty busy.' He said, 'Hi, I'm Jack. You're Stan's wife, right?'"

Later, after Kennedy was elected president, Stan played with Ella Fitzgerald at the Commander in Chief's lavish birthday party on May 19, 1962, when fifteen thousand people filled Madison Square Garden for a gala event that featured Ella alongside other celebrities like Jack Benny and Marilyn Monroe.

"No one was allowed to bring cameras in," said Angela. "But Stan had a movie camera with him in the pit, and he filmed Kennedy coming down the steps with his bodyguards. Stan was standing up to get the picture and as Jack got closer I could see him look at Stan with a little smile on his face, like, 'Oh, you are *so* bad!'"

But it was Marilyn Monroe who was remembered for being naughty that night, with her sewn-on dress and seductive version of "Happy Birthday," which she sang to her rumored lover with piano accompaniment from Hank Jones, one of Stan's old buddies from Fifty-Second Street. The moment was ripe with intrigue in the form of Sam Giancana, the Chicago mob boss and Frank Sinatra pal who reportedly made a deal with Kennedy's father to swing the presidential election by delivering key voting districts in Illinois. Monroe's relationships with Kennedy and Giancana were contemporaneous, and her death occurred only three months after Kennedy's birthday celebration, after a date with Giancana. The Outfit boss became a suspect in both Monroe's death and Kennedy's assassination. All of this contributed to the evening's mystique, and Monroe's dress eventually sold at auction for $1.26 million. The flesh-colored number wasn't the only valuable piece of memorabilia from that famous night. Thirty years later, Stan sold his bootleg film for $25,000.

Stan's next steady gig was one of the choicest jobs in jazz. Ella Fitzgerald was even bigger than Peggy Lee. The homely teenager Stan saw singing with Chick Webb had grown into an international celebrity. Like Billie Holiday, Ella had lived the blues, but unlike Lady Day, she also knew the reality of not being physically beautiful. Ella's talent as a singer was simply so sublime that it transcended the pretty face and figure essential to so many divas. She was loved all over the world, and she treated her musicians very well.

Norman Granz was Ella's manager. He had scabbed over. He knew I had been clean for years, and we became friends, if you can believe it. He called me up. Said Ella wanted a new rhythm section. So I joined up with Paul Smith, a wonderful, fantastic piano player, and Wilfred Middlebrooks, a very fine bass player. We signed a two-year contract. Toured the U.S., Europe, and Canada. It was first class, all the way.

Now, with Ella, you got paid for fifty-two weeks a year, but you only worked what—thirty, thirty-five? I was back here, doing record dates and still getting paid. We flew everywhere, except for Paul. He used to take his Cadillac, and he only ate peanut butter sandwiches on the road, with bread and jelly. No restaurants. He had a briefcase full of Skippy.

The rest of us always flew. One time, coming out of Calgary, we're on a DC-8. Full plane. We're five hundred feet up and *pow!* An engine catches fire. The plane starts to jerk backwards. This is it, for sure.

Somehow, this pilot brought it in. He fought it down. When he came out of the cockpit, he almost had his shirt off. Ella was gray. I hear someone screaming, "Help! Let me out!" She's pounding on the door and it's the stewardess! We thought we were going to eat it that day. Half an hour later, we're on another plane.

One time, we were playing a concert in London at one of the old theaters. We're playing away, swinging. And she's singing. People are loving it. All of a sudden, from the side of the wing, a guy starts to stagger out. He's got a long beard, he's disheveled, and he's staggering out, getting closer and closer, so Ella—me being the bouncer, or whatever—is looking at me. "Do something, do something!" So I stop playing and walk over, and I pick the guy up. He's kind of a small guy. I grab him by the collar and the seat of his pants, and I walk him off the stage, give him a little bump—"Stay off."

I get back on the drums. We're playing again and all of a sudden here he comes again. What is it with this guy? Ella looks at him and does a double take. She stops singing and says, "Ladies and Gentlemen, Montgomery Clift!" The audience applauds him and then they start to boo me because I threw him off the stage, which was very funny.

He takes a bow and then staggers off. It was very sad. He was a mess. Unrecognizable.

In Washington, we shared a bill with the Dave Brubeck Quartet. Joe Morello and I were hanging out the way drummers do, and you know, he's legally blind, or very close. I asked him what his hobbies were. He said, "Target practice," and I said, "Not with me, Joe!"

Ella could be a little temperamental, like most. "How come you're playing so loud?" You know, that type of thing. We placated her. One time we played Philly, and she introduces me as, "Philly's own Stan Levey!" That was real nice. I appreciated that. At Christmastime she gave us beautiful luggage.

She had a lonely life. Never really found a man. She was actually very pretty, in my opinion. What can I say about her singing? What can anyone say? She's like an instrument. Like Charlie Parker without a horn. Incredible sound, incredible interpretation of a lyric, incredible phrasing. And a really, really nice girl. She treated us beautifully.

Working with Peggy and Ella served as a bridge from jazz to popular music. In the early-to-mid-1960s, Stan worked as a low-profile drummer and percussionist for some of the biggest names in show business. In one hour alone, Stan probably reached more ears than he had in his entire jazz career when he played with the Supremes—a planetary sensation at the time—on their 1963 CBS television special. Legions also heard Stan's anonymous drumming on Bobby Darin recordings. Other unlikely artists hired Stan to contribute to their records and performances, including the Beach Boys. Coincidentally, before the Beach Boys became famous, Brian Wilson had been Robert Levey's Pony League baseball coach.

"He did some percussion for them," said David Levey. "They had a home studio in Laurel Canyon—a pot-smoking fest. Bunch of long-haired beach hippies. Dad probably had great disdain for them because they were at best mediocre musicians and probably using drugs up there and drinking, which Dad did not take kindly to. He was as straight as a policeman. Dad was like a cop in his thirties, forties, and fifties. Half a beer on a weekend and that was it. He was absolutely committed to sobriety."

Stan's temperance and devotion to his family were virtues that appealed to Pat Boone, the wholesome entertainer with an enormous following of Christian fans. It was a world away from the dark days in Bird's broom closet.

Pat Boone was a good buddy of mine. He was a sweetheart of a guy. It wasn't jazz, but he was a nice fella. Paul Smith and I played with Pat on lots of dates and we went to Japan together. Had a wonderful trip.

"Dad did a bunch of live stuff with Pat Boone over a couple of years' time," said David. "Especially in New York and Las Vegas. We traveled as a family. Pat would introduce his band, and when he got to Dad he would say, 'And Stan's lovely family is here tonight,' and they would swing out a huge spotlight onto our table and we'd stand up and everyone applauded. That would never happen today. Pat was that kind of a guy. A family man."

CHAPTER 12

HOLLYWOOD STUDIOS

After finishing his two-year contract with Ella Fitzgerald, Stan decided to reinvent himself once again as a full-time studio musician. The competition was fierce, and Stan determined that he would give himself an edge by mastering the mallet instruments: the vibraphone, xylophone, marimba, and timpani. Stan had learned to read fairly well with Kenton, but he now resolved to hone his sight-reading ability and become a finished musician. He hired Emil Richards as an instructor and hit the woodshed.

"He didn't sleep for three weeks," said Angela. "He taught himself to read by working out duets, trios, concertos—everything—on all of his instruments. He even studied composing and orchestration."

My first studio job was with Shorty Rogers. That was back in '54. Shorty was doing a film with a terrible actor. It was a film for Universal. And what was the name of it? *I Got to Live?* Or—no, not that, not that one. Something weird. Anyway, Shorty's band—he hired me to play the movie.

But later, when I really got into it, I played mallets and timpani, and by that time I had pretty good education. You've got to be pretty bright-eyed and bushy-tailed to do that work—8:00 AM, *"Let's go . . . Downbeat!"* You don't make any mistakes. It kept you on your toes. Beethoven, Bach, violin trios, everything. Just read it and record it.

I worked for Universal, Twentieth Century Fox. I worked a lot with Nelson Riddle and Lalo Schifrin, Henry Mancini, André Previn, Neal Hefti. And I did a lot of television—six hours of *Batman* twice a week, *The Munsters, The Addams Family, Laredo, I Dream of Jeannie, Bewitched.* All kinds of stuff.

I did the Johnny Carson show—*The Tonight Show*— every time they came out to L.A., six or seven weeks a year, with the conductor at the time, who was Skitch Henderson. James Coburn comes on the show. He said he was a gong player. He does this weird shtick with his gong, and it's ridiculous. Carson's tapping his pencil . . . rolling his eyes. Then Coburn tells Carson he gets his gong to talk to him. Carson looks over at me and says, "Hey Stan! You get your tom-toms to talk to you, too?" Then they cut to the break. It was the only time he ever spoke to me.

Anyway, it was during one of those *Tonight Show* jobs that I met Frank Sinatra.

Stan and Frank Sinatra had several things in common, including Harry Anslinger, for it was on account of Sinatra that Harry Anslinger kicked Lucky Luciano out of Cuba. The FBN believed the singer had carried millions of dollars of mob money to Havana during a major summit meeting of the national syndicate. Along with the alleged briefcase full of cash, Sinatra brought with him to Havana a gold cigarette lighter inscribed with the words: "To my dear pal Lucky, from his friend, Frank Sinatra."

Anslinger knew Luciano was in Cuba almost immediately

after his arrival. The commissioner's original plan was to keep the mob boss under surveillance and quietly gather intelligence. But by openly fraternizing with Sinatra, Luciano exposed himself to reporters who publicized his presence, which in turn forced Anslinger's hand. Luciano was sent back to Italy, where the Carabinieri later found the gold cigarette lighter while serving a warrant. To Harry Anslinger, the lighter, signed as it was to a mobster from a jazz musician, was an object as loathsome as a cockroach.

I had done some work with him in the studios on commercials and record dates with Nelson Riddle, but he never talked to anyone. So now I'm standing at NBC in a hallway. Frank was doing a show with Jimmy Durante right down the hall in Studio D. And he comes down. You know, he's tired, and he sees me. He came right over to me. He says, "Hey, Stan, how are you?"

And now I'm talking to Frank Sinatra. He says, "I saw you fight in New Jersey. I liked the way you moved. You really handled yourself well." He's a big fight fan. I remember he had some nice moves. We're talking about boxing and everything for about ten, fifteen minutes, you know. Everything's fine and he says, "Okay, see you, Stan."

The next day I'm standing in the hall again and here he comes—my new friend, Frank Sinatra. He walks by, and I say, "Hi Frank, how you doing?" He shouts, "Hey! You don't talk to me! I tell you when to talk!" With the finger in my face, you know.

If Stan imagined how easily he could dump Sinatra, he didn't let on. Stan knew enough about the music business and the mob to know when to bite his tongue. Also unspoken was the other subject the two musicians had in common: Shirley Van Dyke. By the time Stan's first son, Robert, was a teenager, Shirley had given up her ambitions of stardom.

"She was living with this guy," Robert said, "and every day, they would sit around the dining room table and forge payroll checks. They had all these artist's tools. And they would go cash them."

In 1963, the Argentinean composer Lalo Schifrin moved to Hollywood, where he hired Stan for some of his earliest film scores in a body of work that came to include *Cool Hand Luke, Mission: Impossible*, and *The Amityville Horror.*

"I had recordings of Stan already . . . even in Argentina," said Schifrin. "I was big fan of Hampton Hawes and I knew that Stan had played with Charlie Parker, too. When I moved to California, the first thing I thought about when I needed a drummer was Stan Levey. And one of my first movies was *The Cincinnati Kid* with Steve McQueen, where the theme song was sung by Ray Charles, and Stan played on that recording. And then I started to do television . . . for NBC . . . and Stan played all the episodes. Stan played also, my movie *Bullitt*, with Steve McQueen. Everything I did in those days, Stan was my man."

"Stan and Ray Charles didn't exactly gel," said Robert Levey. "Ray played a lot looser and with a wider beat . . . not the way Stan played. Not his favorite guy to work with."

Stan appreciated the quality, the money, and the prestige, but he found the nuts and bolts of studio work to be stressful and stifling. Fortunately, live jazz offered an outlet and Stan subbed around L.A. when he could. One such gig was a short-lived quintet with Terry Gibbs, Conte Candoli, Russ Freeman, and a young Charlie Haden on bass. A two-week stint with George Shearing's band included newcomer Gary

Burton on vibraphone.

"Stan was one of the first people I met in the jazz field who seemed to have a life beyond music," Burton remembered.

Stan also teamed up with some Hollywood friends to form a leisure band that brought welcome relief from the slogging drudgery of studio work.

"They did it for fun and because the music was good," said Angela. "They were just mischievous and crazy and ridiculous together."

Trumpeter and vocalist Jack Sheldon was the titular leader of the band, which also included Joe Mondragon on bass, Howard Roberts on guitar, and Jack Marshall arranging, composing, and doubling on guitar. Sheldon was Merv Griffin's comic foil on prime-time television, and that's his voice on *Schoolhouse Rock!* cartoons like "Conjunction Junction" and "I'm Just a Bill." Sheldon also played his evocative trumpet with Kenton and, later, Tom Waits. Jack Marshall was a record producer and a gifted composer who wrote the alluring arrangement to "Fever" that Stan played with Peggy Lee, as well as many other irresistible songs like the madcap theme to *The Munsters.*

We had a little jazz band. Did jobs around here just for fun and in San Francisco at the Trident, where we had quite a following. We had a wonderful camaraderie. Sol Saks was a writer, and he would come along. Jack Marshall had four children, including Frank. We were like uncles to Frank. Now he's got Academy Awards for producing all the best movies, working with Steven Spielberg and Frank's wife, who is Kathleen Kennedy.

"It was great having him in the band because he was this

big boxer, so nobody would ever fool with [us]," Sheldon joked about Stan. "We always got paid. Stan would never have to do anything, just stand in the corner and make a face."

The band even made an album. *Jack Sheldon: Live at Don Mupo's Gold Nugget* doesn't take itself too seriously, but it has some sizzling moments. The band's playful brand of semi-sarcasm helped release the tension built up from working overtime in the studios, where Stan eventually played on thousands of television episodes and hundreds of film scores.

"We loved tagging along," said Stan's son, Chris. "We went to a number of his recordings as kids. I remember the big boom microphones and being frightened to death I might cough or move my foot. For some reason, the *Paint Your Wagon* session made a big impression on me. It was at RCA. I was developing an interest in the bass, and I remember watching Max Bennett. Then I'd go in the booth and see how they worked the engineering. These guys were somewhere between mechanical and scientific, and very accurate about what they produced, so it was pretty impressive. It was a fairly elite club to belong to."

The money was good and Stan became a complete musician, but the work brought little in the way of enjoyment.

What's to enjoy? You go in at eight, nine in the morning, and don't make any mistakes. "Let's go!" Read it and record it.

It was tough, tough work. There's no joy in doing studio work. I'd be running from timpani, to the xylophone, back to the chimes, all with the headset, the click track going. Don't fall. Get in on cue. It's not music, it's sound effects. Just cues and bridges, bridges and cues: "*Fourteeen seconds!*" That kind of thing. It'll put you in the nuthouse.

One time I'm doing a Barbra Streisand record for Dick

Hazard. I'm playing vibraphone. She says, "Wait a minute." She's looking back at me. "Can I hear what you're playing?" She says, "That's not right."

I know it's not right, but it's what's there on the paper and that's what I have to play. I knew it wasn't right, but I'm not going to change that note because I'm brainwashed into doing what's there. That's studio work. It'll turn you into one of those crazy bastards I used to hold down in prison.

Mission: Impossible and *Mannix* were kind of fun, drumistically. Very percussive. Challenging, you know, and Lalo did both of those.

The money was great, but you're on a day rate with the government. They take half your money right up front. I said, "Man, I can make more money than this easier."

This studio guy started shoving things up the tubes of my vibraphone. I'm saying, "What the hell are you doing? Get outta here." He says, "Hey, just play the instrument. Let me take care of this." On the playback it came out sounding like a cello. I could see what was coming. Everything would be electronic, and they wouldn't need me anymore. I said, "No, I can't go for this." You know, they brought in a synthesizer —just starting. I said, "Let me outta here!"

CHAPTER 13

LIFE AFTER MUSIC

In 1973, when Stan finished work on the soundtrack to *Rosemary's Baby*, he put down his sticks, walked away, and never played the drums again.

"It didn't seem like he gave it months of thought," Angela said. "It was just, 'This is how I feel, and I feel it's right, so that's what I'm going to do.' I never questioned or doubted his decision. I just accepted it. He kept a lot of things to himself. He didn't want to be a whiner, I guess, but I think it had a lot to do with his hands. His hands were drawn up permanently from this thick, disfiguring scarring occurring deep in his palms. That was difficult, I think."

The abruptness and finality of Stan's decision was a source of fascination to everyone but himself. "People constantly questioned him," said Angela. "Right up until the end, people would say, 'How could you just walk away and never play music again?' He never explained himself. He'd say, 'I just did.'"

At the time of his break with music, Stan was bent on sending his sons, Chris and David, to medical school. His photography business was doing well, but it still seemed like a huge risk compared to the good money he'd been making as a studio musician. But Stan insisted he couldn't afford *not* to break away.

"We'd go into the musicians' union," said Chris, "sometimes to cash a check or just to see some of the other cats. He'd say, 'Some of the most talented players in the world are sitting in the back room, begging for a gig. I don't want to be one of them.' Nobody could fault him. He had a lot of pride."

> They wanted younger musicians. I could see the handwriting on the wall. You get used up. You get used up and thrown out. I didn't want to end up wearing a shiny blue suit doing club work. I knew I had to do it, and I just did it. Like everything else I did, I just did it. Never regretted it.

Stan's photography business was a natural segue from the music industry. "He morphed into it," said Chris. "After the jazz and studio stuff started to wane, he played a lot of casuals: weddings, bar mitzvahs, that type of thing. From a musical standpoint, he hated it, but he networked and got to know the people who organized parties and events, so it was a natural progression."

"He always had a camera with him," said Angela. "He'd take a picture and producers would say, 'Maybe we can use that for a cover.' He had that in the back of his mind and he liked it. Musical people would ask him about layout and design, and then drum companies and cymbal companies started hiring him."

Stan's album covers and music advertisements augmented the weddings, bar mitzvahs, and other events that became his bread and butter. When his developer ruined a whole wedding's worth of negatives, Stan decided to develop his own. "He built a big color lab and studio off the kitchen," Angela said. "Learning it was very difficult. He wouldn't sleep. He'd just stare and read until he mastered it. He was always that way with everything. He'd study it and then he'd have it."

"Everything he's ever done, he did with his two hands," said David. "Boxing, drumming, photography. Everything, self-taught. He came into photography at a good time. Not everyone's Uncle Harry had a digital camera in his back pocket."

My sons were thrilled that I was a drummer. I'd take them to record dates. They loved it, but when they said they wanted to be musicians, I said, "Man, I'll shoot you first." Robert and David are drummers and Chris is a bass player. They were heading for music. You know the band Toto? They started right here in my garage.

"In high school," David said, "my very best buddies—Steve 'Luke' Lukather, the Porcaro brothers, particularly Steve, who was my age, joined by John Pierce and Mike Landau—were some of the guys that went on to create the band Toto. For two or three years, if I wasn't sleeping over at Steve's house, he was sleeping at mine. We were in our practice studio for hours upon hours every day, perfecting our craft. Shortly after I stood up from the drum chair to go to college, one of my heroes, drummer Jeff Porcaro, sat down, and that was Toto."

Toto's jazz lineage has been obscured by their enormous success in arena rock, but they were products of, and participants in, the West Coast jazz scene: the Porcaro brothers are the sons of Stan's percussion colleague Joe Porcaro; keyboardist David Paich is the son of Marty Paich, a former Lighthouse All-Star whom Stan considered one of the best arrangers in the business; guitarist Steve Lukather was called on to play with none other than Miles Davis; and Toto's fingerprints are all over jazz-infused recordings by Quincy Jones, Steely Dan, Boz Scaggs, George Benson, Larry Carlton, and others.

"Stan didn't want anybody to be a musician," said Steve

Lukather. "Especially Chris and David. He didn't want to show any excitement for it. We didn't know about any of the darkness he'd been through earlier in his life. We didn't even know he was this heavy, legendary bebop cat until later on. Stan was an intense presence. He had a soft side, but when he walked into a room he commanded respect. He and Angie were going out one night and he said, 'You boys better not be doing any bullshit here! No goofing around—and you *know* what I mean!' So they left the raging teenagers at home and we probably went out and got some beers or something, and they came back home early and we got caught red-handed. Got kicked out of the practice studio. I seem to remember all of us coming back and groveling for forgiveness.

"We always wanted him to play for us. We'd bug him. 'C'mon, Mr. Levey, let's hear you throw down a little bit!' We saw him sit down once and play. He starts fooling around and just when it was starting to get amazing, he said, 'Aww . . . I don't do this anymore,' and he got up."

"I went off to college, and one day I'm driving to organic chemistry class," David said. "I turn on the radio and *boom*— 'Hold the Line!' Yes! *Yes!* My boys did it! Well, *Toto* went platinum, became a household name, and the rest, as the say, is history."

David also played with top jazz cats like Art Pepper and Dexter Gordon, and even toured with Davy Jones and the Monkees.

Chris, the bassist of the family, played many of the best clubs in Los Angeles, gigging with cats like Chris Pinnick and Kevin Dubrow of Quiet Riot. Chris played live with Dionne Warwick and the Coasters and found plenty of work in the studios, where he recorded a few tunes with Burt Bacharach and laid down tracks for commercials and television. "I was always subbing for somebody," said Chris. "I was going to school the whole time, but I supported myself with music."

Robert played on the Sunset Strip in the late '60s and early '70s, and recorded for the dance show *Boss City* with Jeannie Brown. He also appeared with the Outlaw Blues Band on the cult record *Breaking In*, which was produced by Bob Thiele of Coltrane fame. Years later, Robert's drum work on the track "Deep Gully" was sampled by both Cyprus Hill and De La Soul. In 2009, Robert released his first CD as a bandleader, a jazz outing called *Homey* that would've made the old man proud. One of Robert's oldest friends, Little Feat guitarist Paul Barrere, contributed to the liner notes. Barrere and Robert were part of a circle of high school friends that included Leroy Vinnegar's two sons Mark and Kevin, and Red Rodney's son Mark Rodney.

You can always play your music, I told them. Best hobby in the world. I just don't want you to get serious. David got crazy and moved to Aspen. Long hair down his back. We gave up on him. Eight months later, the doorbell rings.

"I think I want to go back to school . . . "

"Okay, come in. We'll talk about it. Get a haircut, and don't hurt your mother."

In addition to his own sons, Stan was known to be generous to other young men who were drawn to him—guys like Hoagy Carmichael Jr. and drummer John Guerin, who was a regular at the twelve-hour Sunday Lighthouse sessions and marveled at Stan's ability to play fast tempos "forever." Another was the son of Ellis Tollin, who drifted into California a troubled soul.

"He helped him out when he needed it," said Angela.

"Stan was like that with everybody. Everybody loved him. *Loved, loved, loved* him. Everywhere I'd go, people would say, 'I just love your husband!' I told Stan, 'I'm so sick of people telling me how much they love you.' He's always quick with a joke. He said, 'I know . . . you're the only one that doesn't.'"

Late in life, and in spite of his eighth-grade education, Stan developed an interest in space and physics. "That led him to become more spiritual," said David, "wondering, 'What does it all mean?'" Stan searched for answers through transcendental meditation, a discipline he engaged in with the same commitment he showed to sobriety. "He meditated every day," Angela said. "It really worked for him."

Unfortunately, though, it couldn't prevent a malignant tumor from developing at the base of Stan's tongue. The standard of care in 1988 was surgery with a six-percent, five-year survival rate. Those who endured the procedure were left with visible scars on the face and neck and sometimes the disfiguring condition of shoulder drop. The UCLA Medical Center was initiating a study for radiation-only treatment, and Stan eagerly qualified.

In the '80s, Buddy Rich got very sick. About '87, he was playing in New York and his arm flew up in the air. No control.

[Buddy] flew back to UCLA. We all got the news. Tumor. I went down to the hospital three times a week and helped walk him up and down the halls. His left arm was dead. His leg went dead. Pitiful. Here he is in bed. We really loved the guy. He'd go down to radiation and I would go down sometimes to keep him company when he had to lay under the machine.

It got worse and worse. Finally, he said, "Don't send me home half-done. Give me the operation. If I make it, fine. If not, okay." They gave him the operation and sent him home to a friend's house. Armenian guy. Buddy died there. I was one of the pallbearers. Alvin Stoller, myself, and Irv Cottler were drummer pallbearers. The setting was beautiful. Flowers were placed on either side of the closed casket. In front—one of Buddy's drum sets. Sinatra gave the eulogy. Carson came to the microphone and completely broke up crying.

About one year later, I wind up in UCLA and I'm laying under the same machine. I walked into UCLA with a stage four cancer, base of the tongue right down to here, man. Bye-bye. Dr. Calcaterra and Dr. Julliard, they kept me alive, those guys. Calcaterra said, "Well, you're a goner. You'd better finish up your business unless you let me operate." I said, "You ain't touching me." My kids flew in. "You've got to have it, Dad. You've got to have the operation."

I don't have to have anything, and I didn't. I just went downstairs to radiation—radiology, and Julliard personally worked on me. He's the head of it. They gave me seven thousand rads. Eight thousand, you turn into a toad. And that's why I chew. I don't have any—they burned my saliva glands out. I was in bed for seven months, hanging in.

Stan "lived to suffer from it." His face and neck were badly burnt, and he became dependent on his water bottle and chewing gum. His photography business was never the same, and he found himself retiring against his will—a source of considerable depression for the workaholic.

Nevertheless, he was proud of being a cancer survivor, and he was buoyed by Angela, who approached Stan's illness with an optimism that her son David couldn't help but view as denial in light of the statistics. Her "everything's going to be fine" attitude helped Stan stay positive and motivated. He compared being a cancer survivor—the pain and suffering, the determination and endurance—to being in the boxing ring. Still, he was reticent to say that he'd beat cancer. "He never took that for granted," said Chris. "He respected the veracity of malignancies."

By the 1990s, Stan was a "forgotten man of jazz," in the words of Leonard Feather. Occasionally, a request for an interview came, more often as not from the U.K. Actor Forest Whitaker came calling and spent nearly two days holed up in Stan's studio, probing the old drummer's memory in preparation for his role as Charlie Parker in Clint Eastwood's film *Bird*. Ken Burns also sought Stan out and included him in several episodes of his epic film documentary *Jazz: A History of America's Music*. Stan always obliged the inevitable Parker questions but also seemed to enjoy steering the conversation to some of the other forgotten cats he'd played with: Boyd Raeburn, Clyde Hart, Ziggy Vines . . . Stan did little to stem his own anonymity, and in fact encouraged it with his own modesty.

Bill Lynch developed a friendship with Stan after moving into the Levey's Sherman Oaks neighborhood in the late 1980s. A professional guitarist from the musically fertile town of Lawrence, Kansas, Lynch had played with many stars, including Bird's old boss, Jay McShann—yet he had no idea who Stan was.

"In the fourteen years that I knew him, he never once mentioned his music," Lynch said. "He described himself as a mostly retired photographer, and that's what I knew him as. After he died, a friend of mine called and said, 'Hey Bill, I see your neighbor died.' I said, 'Well how in the world would you know that my neighbor died?' He said, 'I read it in the paper—you mean you didn't know who he was?' In dozens and dozens of conversations, Stan never brought up what he had done. You'd think if you did all that, you'd tell everyone."

By the time Stan's throat cancer recurred in 2003, he had also endured prostate cancer and a five-artery bypass. Film and stage director Stu Berg met Stan in cardiac rehab, where a group of men who had gone through open-heart surgery joked that they were the "Zipper Club." The Zipper Club met three times a week for lunch after their rehab sessions.

"Stan was fighter," Berg said. "He never complained, and he always said he was 'lucky to be here, plain and simple.' He didn't dwell on it. Stan was just one of the guys, until one time when we walked into a restaurant where Louie Bellson was eating. You'd have thought the president had arrived, the way Louie Bellson got up and rushed over to Stan and threw his arms around him. Another time, we went to the fiftieth anniversary party for Capitol Records and it was the same thing all night long, with musician after musician paying homage to Stan. He was a little shy when people would make a fuss over him."

One such occasion occurred when Stan and Angela flew back to D.C. for one of her nephew's weddings in 1997. Angela was perusing a local paper and saw that Lenny Garment, President Nixon's lawyer and Stan's old bandmate, was doing a presentation and book signing for *Crazy Rhythm* the next evening in Chevy Chase, at the All Saints Episcopal Church. Stan and Angela arrived early enough to get seats in the front row.

"He was up there talking for a minute, and his eyes fell on Stan and he almost fell off the podium," said Angela. "'My God, is that Stan Levey sitting there?' He was laughing and pointing. They ended up having such a long conversation that the audience started to get annoyed. Finally Stan says, 'Gee,

Lenny, I think they want to hear about Nixon, not me.'"
Garment signed Stan's copy of *Crazy Rhythm*:

> To Stan Levey, who knows as much, or more, than I do
> about "Crazy Rhythm." What a treat: all the years of
> funny people, funny "not sad" moments and the rest
> came back when you "appeared" in All Saints Epis-
> copal Church today. Halleluiah! (In the key of "?")
> Love, Lenny Garment.

Drugs, discrimination, violence, poverty, and prison were all part of the boxing and jazz life, and the competition was fierce. Many of Stan's fellow boxers and beboppers died young, but Stan was a survivor—one of the only jazz junkies to break free from the ravages of heroin. He overcame addiction, prison, and an eighth-grade education with a dose of talent and a ton of hard work. In the process, he transformed himself from a self-taught kid playing backwards into a finished musician, and from a thieving junkie into a solid citizen and family man.

Stan bridged the old-school, rough-and-tumble jazz culture with the newer version of a fine art generally uncluttered with depravity—a scene closer to the concert hall than the smoky clubs of the underworld. Today's professional jazz musicians struggle even harder than earlier generations to make a living, yet they are more likely to have a college degree than a heroin habit. With virtuosity unmarred by Bird-like behavior, today's stars are by and large excellent role models. Stan saw this as a positive development, and admired Wynton Marsalis. "He's given it a real boost up, you know," he said. "I think it's a good image." Joshua Redman also impressed Stan, even though the Harvard grad chose jazz over Yale Law School. "He can really play!" he said.

Still, there was something to be said for the old days.

We used very minimal equipment. We had a bass drum, a snare, a tom-tom—maybe two tom-toms—a ride cymbal, and high hat. Maybe a small cut cymbal. We didn't need much more because we had to make do. The young drummers are miraculous. The reasons are not difficult to find. There's more music available to them. Every kid's got drums. Every kid's got a teacher. They have cassettes; they have videotapes. It's all there, you know. Every garage has a drum set. Yes, they're using more drums and cymbals today, but they're *using* them. It's not just a matter of cosmetics. The number of cymbals and drums that make up a set today is apropos of young players' technique and ability.

Now, in those days, we had absolutely nothing. I believe in studying. But as far as drumming goes, don't overemphasize the academic side of things. Learn to read properly. Learn to interpret what you see on the paper. Take those black dots, those notes, and make them into music. If you combine practice and study with on-the-job training, the results generally are quite good. You develop "chops" while getting close to music and understanding it. It's mostly by listening and watching others play.

I was completely self-taught because we couldn't afford a teacher, and that's why I play left-handed, even though I am right-handed. We had zero. I got my education on the street, which a lot of people did in those days, you know. That went for music, too. No books or videos. No records, hardly. You had to wait for a band to come in maybe twice a year, try to get a look at the drummer, see what he's doing. There was no information anywhere, which maybe makes it better. Makes you work harder, I think.

Hard work. The woodshed. In the end, it distinguished Stan even more than his natural talent.

"Even if the sun did not rise on a given day, my dad would still be up, toiling in his office, making something happen," David said. "During the slow times, when work was dry . . . Mom said, 'Boys, things are not working out very well right now . . . nothing is certain. We may have to batten down the hatches.' But Dad would stay busy no matter what. When he practiced on the vibraphone and xylophone, it was for eight, ten, twelve hours at a time. He was industrious on a daily basis, regardless if he had work that day or not. He applied woodshedding to everyone: doctors, lawyers, everyone. When I was in college and medical school, you can be damn sure that's exactly what I was doing—woodshedding."

"He always had a punching bag set up, and he was always working out on it," said Chris. "A speed bag . . . his hands and feet all going in a little dance. I can still hear it. A lot of triplets going on there."

"Stan took care of everything with the house," said Angela. "He was obsessed with leaf blowers, and he had a couple of them. One day, I came home and he'd had wrought-iron railing installed. I said, 'Stan, it looks like an old folks' home!' He said, 'I got news for you. It is!' It kills me that I didn't appreciate it enough. I was able to stay at home, and I enjoyed every minute of it. It makes me want to tell all the women I meet, 'Appreciate what your husband does.'"

Angela did go to work when the boys were much older. She drew on Stan's studio contacts and the acting talent she had acquired as a girl in the drama department at Catholic University to land day player parts in movies and television. Angela appeared in episodes of *The Nanny*, *Six Feet Under*, *Thirtysomething*, *Rude Awakening*, *True Lies*, and close to fifty commercials.

"Nobody ever heard of me, which is what both Stan and I wanted," she said. "It was very hard work—twelve to sixteen hours a day."

Welcome to the woodshed.

So in February of 2003, I get a call from someone named Krupnick. He said, "Well, I'm the advance man for the Rolling Stones." Right away, I think the guy's putting me on.

"Okay, what's the gag?"

He says, "Well, Charlie Watts wants to come out and meet you."

Charlie Watts.

Well, I had seen the band on television. It's not my thing—you know, a two-chord band—but they do a great show and they have that underlying swing, you know. And Charlie. I kept looking at Charlie on the TV, and I said, "This guy can really play the drums!" Of course, he fit with them. He really held it together. He was a real glue guy. He glued it in there. He locked it in. Beautiful!

I said, "Well, are you putting me on or what?"

He said, "No. They want to come out and meet you. They've got a concert. They want you to come to the concert."

We made a date and a time, and the limo pulls up and Charlie comes in with Jim Keltner and Charlie and I just hugged each other. It was really weird. It was like we were old brothers or something, you know. It was like when Charlie Parker smiled at me with that gold-rimmed tooth.

We went in my room, and I got all these pictures of Bird and he went nuts. So I made him computer printouts—good copy—and he went crazy. And I gave him records he hadn't heard—Victor Feldman—guys like that who can really play. They had lunch here. We had a great time.

That night they played a "job" at the Staples Center, and we went VIP with the limo. Ex-President Clinton was there. Names, names . . . the leader? Mick Jagger! Mick Jagger came by, and Keith Richards. Great guys. They all knew me. I said, "My God, I'm prehistoric, man. You guys think you're in a museum here."

Charlie? We're going to be friends until the end, I can tell you. We're locked in.

On April 19, 2005, the drummer's heart sounded it's final beat. Stan was seventy-nine. He was honored with a *New York Times* obituary written by noted jazz critic Peter Keepnews. Hundreds attended his memorial service, and Stan was interred in a mausoleum at the sprawling Forest Lawn Cemetery, where Angela visited afterward almost every day, walking through a gauntlet of deceased celebrities en route to Stan's resting place—Bette Davis, Liberace, Morey Amsterdam, and friends like Bobby Darin and Julie London. On one such visit, Angela and David made a delightful discovery: Stan's mother was buried just outside his mausoleum.

My three sons are my proudest achievement. Chris and David are both top radiologists, and Robert is a master painter. I'm very lucky. See, Angela was like an old-time Sicilian wife. That was her life, those boys.

Robert credits Angela for helping to save him from the ruin wrought by his own mother. "Boy, did she put up with a lot from me," he said of his stepmother. "But she always treated me like I was her son. A couple of times, Dad tried to bail me out of life with my mother, but he was rigid—military—and I wasn't going for that. I was crazy. I really looked up to my old man, almost too much, and I really loved him, but I never listened to him and Angela. I got sent to juvie for grand theft auto and fighting. I got on heroin at about seventeen. I had a lot of anger . . . I was psycho. I made knives, hit people with chains. I liked to fight. I didn't mind it. I beat up my mother once. I was a man of my emotions."

Stan and Robert's relationship remained tempestuous into Robert's adulthood, which included a ten-year separation from his father. "Later on we mended things up," said Robert. "Besides Yeshua, it was he and Angela who saved me, in a lot of ways. In the end he said, 'Robert, you're okay,' but I wish we could've shared more, some of my accomplishments . . . that type of thing."

Much to Stan's satisfaction, Robert finally channeled his angst into the woodshed, apprenticing himself to a master craftsman from England, who taught him the painstaking arts of wood graining, faux marbling, and other highly skilled finishing techniques in the European tradition. Located in Western Colorado, Bob Levey Decorative Finishing boasts a long list of celebrity clients and public buildings all over the country. One of the more auspicious projects for the jazz scion was the restoration of the Gershwin Piano, now on display at the Library of Congress. Robert is a Fourth Degree Black Belt in Tae Kwon Do and deeply spiritual man, a Messianic Jew whose faith is reflected in the name of his group. The Intervention Band includes multi-instrumentalist Tim Fox, and plays the finest jazz between Denver and Salt Lake City. Bob has a daughter, Kristen, and two sons, Anthony and Joseph. He is endorsed by Soultone Cymbals, which he plays in a kit that includes one of Stan's old snares.

Dr. Christopher Levey went to medical school on a Navy scholarship, serving two years as a general practitioner on the USS Sylvania out of Norfolk, Virginia and two more years at Camp LeJeune, North Carolina. Chris now practices diagnostic radiology in Easton, Maryland. He and his wife Kate have three children: Erica, Danny, and Suzanna. Chris plays electric bass in a diverse array of ensembles including an eighteen-piece big band, a church group, and several jazz and Americana combos.

Dr. David Levey specializes in diagnostic radiology in San Antonio, Texas, where he lives with his daughter Tara. David finds time to play an occasional gig with Johnny P. and the Wiseguys, a crew of flamekeeping cats whose swinging sounds and gangster chic are straight out of the pages of a Stan Levey biography. David also maintains his lifelong friendship with his beloved bandmates in Toto, remaining their most dedicated fan and occasionally joining them on tour in faraway places like Iceland, Mexico, and continental Europe. In 2007, the drummer sat in with the band in Bogotá, Columbia, playing "Hold the Line" for twenty thousand screaming fans.

Stan fought the good fight and came out a winner. As a working-class Jew of his time, place, and lot in life, he might well have ended up a leg-breaker for the mob, playing dismal gigs at girlie joints and channeling his earnings right back to the gangsters through his addiction. But after prison, Stan never used drugs again, and he remained grateful to the criminal justice system for the rest of his life. He proved himself as a husband and a father, and he left behind a legacy as a bebop pioneer and a master of modern rhythm. His drumming career is filled with the mercurial irony typical of jazz. He was the understated speed demon—the cymbal-breaking brute who played quietly.

I was never into the show business end of it. No theatrics for me. My style was helping, contributing. I guess the way I played had a lot to do with my attitude. I was determined to make a contribution and do my job well. I sat down and did my job, played time and made the other musicians feel good.

"Played time" is putting it modestly. Stan was famous for his in-your-face timekeeping, that slashing cymbal beat and buoyant lift that propelled a band forward like the flow of a surfer's wave.

"You could set your watch to his time," said Victor Feldman. "It was one less thing for me to think about when I was playing."

"Stan's time is alive," said Louie Bellson. "It has a pulse that you can always feel."

"That time was the most important thing," said Terry Gibbs. "He'd just sit there and lay it down—give you that time. A soloist could run free. Before I knew it, I had played thirty extra choruses, it felt so good."

Perhaps Dizzy Gillespie said it best when he told Bob Cooper about hiring Stan for a record date in Los Angeles: "We can't let all that good time go to waste."

Stan knew it. In a tongue-in-cheek way of giving himself a compliment, he once said, "Max don't keep the best time, you know."

Perhaps it all harkened back to a young boy and his clock: "*One-two-three, one-two-three, FOUR!*"

RECOMMENDED LISTENING

This section examines a small sampling of Stan Levey's discography, focusing on records for which he took on a leadership role, as well as some noteworthy sideman dates.

DIZZY GILLESPIE, *DIZZY GILLESPIE 1945–1946*
(Classic Records, 1997)

Trumpet: Dizzy Gillespie
Alto saxophone: Charlie Parker
Tenor saxophone: Lucky Thompson and Don Byas
Piano: Al Haig and George Handy
Bass: Ray Brown
Vibraphone: Milt Jackson
Drums: Stan Levey and Sid Catlett

The original Dial session (the date Bird missed in California) is on this record, including, thanks to our good fortune, a rehearsal track from the previous day when Parker was present—the only studio recording of Stan and Bird together. The antique sound quality is a bit of an obstacle to twenty-first-century ears, but the playing cuts through, and the pure, authentic bebop is essential to historians and serious collectors.

STAN KENTON ORCHESTRA, *THE EUROPEAN TOUR 1953*
(Artistry Records, 1997)

Piano: Stan Kenton
Vocals: June Christy
Trumpets: Conte Candoli, Buddy Childress, Don Dennis,
Don Smith, and Ziggy Minichiello
Saxophones: Zoot Sims, Lee Konitz, Bill Holman, Davey
Schildkraut, and Tony Ferina
Trombones: Frank Rosolino, Bill Russo, Keith Moon, Bob
Burgess, and Bill Smiley
Guitar: Barry Galbraith
Bass: Don Bagley
Drums: Stan Levey

*"Levey's glory moment on record with the Kenton band came
on the evening of September 18, 1953, during a concert at the
Alhambra in Paris. He reached a peak level on 'Zoot,' a lean
Bill Holman feature for the gifted tenor man Zoot Sims. Levey
creates an exciting atmosphere for the tenor man and the band.
More than anything, the band and the soloist remind this listener of an excellent, well-conditioned boxer. They feint and punch,
keep moving, building to one climax after another."*

—Burt Korall,
Drummin' Men: The Heartbeat of Jazz: The Bebop Years

When Stan and Angela lived in Hermosa Beach, a man named
Red Clyde came knocking. Clyde was an executive produc-
er for Bethlehem Records, a label associated with artists like
Oscar Pettiford, Charles Mingus, Nina Simone, and Roland
Kirk. Clyde's pitch to Stan was simple: he could record what-
ever he wanted with whomever he wanted, and Clyde would

not interfere. Many of Stan's friends were signing to the label, and working for Bethlehem also included the added bonus of recording with one of the top sound engineers in the business.

One of my old friends is Bones Howe, a producer and sound engineer. He handled many big rock dates, and movies and jazz dates, too. He knows how to set up a band, and he's a great engineer. He was also a drummer. He did quite a few of my albums. He could really mix the sound. He had a good ear, and he knew what the balance should be.

Red Clyde was a drummer, too, at one time. A real nice guy, and he let you do what you wanted to do. Didn't bother you.

We made a quality product. The proof is that you can still buy these records today.

STAN LEVEY, *STAN LEVEY PLAYS THE COMPOSITIONS OF BILL HOLMAN, BOB COOPER, AND JIMMY GIUFFRE*
(Bethlehem Records, 1954)

Tenor saxophone: Zoot Sims
Baritone saxophone: Jimmy Giuffre
Trumpet: Conte Candoli
Piano: Claude Williamson
Bass: Max Bennett
Drums: Stan Levey

Stan made his first album—a ten-inch LP for Bethlehem—in 1954. Reissues like *West Coasting* have compensated for the abbreviated length by pairing it with a Conte Candoli session from the same period; an unnecessary bonus considering how well Levey's record stands on its own. Stan made a statement by eschewing jazz standards and drawing instead from the writing talent of his friends on the coast. The album featured six fresh tunes by Bill Holman, Bob Cooper, and the multi-textured Jimmy Giuffre, who epitomized cool jazz with his cerebral and contrapuntal compositions.

Adventurous arrangements and crack execution made for a hard-hitting debut. Stan's drum parts are explosive and exciting, and his timekeeping slashes like a whip. The band is boisterous but tightly controlled, and the album is packed with ideas and wry fun.

Stan is the star soloist, but his old friend Zoot Sims contributes the fluent, joyful tenor work he was famous for. A native Californian of dirt-poor Okie stock, Sims had played the Central Avenue scene in Los Angeles even before joining Benny Goodman as a teenager in 1942. By the time of this album, he was developing a coast-to-coast reputation as the hardest-swinging and most energizing tenor man on the scene.

"I loved Zoot," said Angela. "He would come to the house a nervous wreck. That was his personality—kind of ADD. He'd come in, wouldn't sit down, talking, laughing . . . The guys in that era, they were so full of music that they didn't really know how to be social. It wasn't in their repertoire, growing up. To get to that level, like Zoot, who was one of the greatest players ever, as far as I'm concerned, you can't really think of much besides music."

STAN LEVEY, *THIS TIME THE DRUM'S ON ME*
(reissued under the title *Stanley the Steamer*)
(Bethlehem Records, 1955)

Tenor saxophone: Dexter Gordon
Trumpet: Conte Candoli
Trombone: Frank Rosolino
Piano: Lou Levy
Bass: Leroy Vinnegar
Drums: Stan Levey

For his second album, Stan brought in Dexter Gordon, his old pal from Harlem and one of the only guys in jazz as physically imposing as himself. Standing six-and-a-half feet tall, the tenor saxophonist had a sound to match his size. Solid and unwavering, Gordon's muscular tone was like the purring of some mighty lion—the sound of the last man standing at every jam session.

Gordon was fresh off a two-year stint in Chino for heroin possession. He was grateful to Stan for a paying gig and a chance to regain lost ground. He even wrote a song for the occasion: "Stanley the Steamer" is a medium-tempo, twelve-bar blues that served the dual purpose of a tribute to Stan and a comeback feature for Gordon in the form of an inspired solo that helped reaffirm his status as a top tenor man. Gordon's biographer, Stan Britt, admired how the saxophonist didn't flinch under the "murderous tempo established by Levey" on the bebop burner "This Time the Drum's On Me." It was a standard that Stan and Gordon had played together in the Spotlite Sextet with Bird and Miles Davis back in the '40s, and Stan used it here to feature his longest solo on record—a two-minute tour de force of earthy strength and scowling intensity.

STAN LEVEY, *GRAND STAN*
(Bethlehem Records, 1956)

Trumpet: Conte Candoli
Tenor saxophone: Richie Kamuca
Trombone: Frank Rosolino
Piano: Sonny Clark
Bass: Leroy Vinnegar
Drums: Stan Levey

"I had this album when I still lived in England in 1957. It's fabulous. Stan had the greatest sound. He had a great feel, medium or fast tempos. Stan's ride beat was so relaxed. Probably the technique he used. He was my idol in the '50s and the early '60s."

—Drummer Colin Bailey

Sonny Clark wasn't as mature a soloist as Zoot Sims or Dexter Gordon, but Stan knew a rising star when he heard one. Clark would later move to New York and become the hottest bop pianist since Bud Powell. His fans will delight in the young man's assertive contributions to *Grand Stan*, including two original compositions. And strap on your seatbelt for Stan's solo on "Hit That Thing," a flowing drum piece that reaches through the speakers and pulls the listener into the swirling depths of Stan's most expansive album. His exit stings with precision, and one's left with the feeling that Stan, who didn't like to take drum solos, needn't have played another one ever again. Rosolino is on fire, and Richie Kamuca sails like a catamaran on the Sonny Clark original "Angel Cake."

Grand Stan has proved so durable that Verse Records reissued it in 2014, almost sixty years after it was recorded.

HOWARD RUMSEY'S LIGHTHOUSE ALL-STARS, MUSIC FOR LIGHTHOUSEKEEPING
(Contemporary Records, 1956)

Bass: Howard Rumsey
Tenor saxophone: Bob Cooper
Trombone: Frank Rosolino
Trumpet: Conte Candoli
Piano: Sonny Clark
Drums: Stan Levey

One of the best of the many Lighthouse records that Stan played on. A young Sonny Clark, a couple of hot Latin numbers, and an excellent solo from Stan on "Love Me or Levey" all make it hard not to love this album.

STAN GETZ QUARTET, *THE STEAMER*
(Verve Records, 1956)

Tenor saxophone: Stan Getz
Piano: Lou Levy
Bass: Leroy Vinnegar
Drums: Stan Levey

Getz had planted a flag a year earlier with *West Coast Jazz*, a classic, barefoot-on-the-beach album with Shelly Manne on drums. *The Steamer* is even better. Here, Getz blossoms fully into his own, unfurling the magnificent tone that earned him the lofty title "The Sound." Oscar Peterson hung the "Steamer" nickname on Getz about the same time Dexter Gordon gave it to Levey.

The two Stanleys cook their way through an up-tempo set seasoned with one minty ballad, and, on "There'll Never Be Another You," an audio spectacle of Levey trading climactic fours with Getz. The effect is a miniature battle in which the boxer steamrolls the sound with a series of stinging breaks that offer up some of Stan's punchiest stick work as a sideman. Had the exchange been a contest for bragging rights to the nickname, the title of "Stanley the Steamer" would no doubt belong to Levey.

CHET BAKER AND ART PEPPER, *THE ROUTE*
(Pacific Jazz, 1956)

Trumpet: Chet Baker
Alto saxophone: Art Pepper
Tenor saxophone: Richie Kamuca
Piano: Pete Jolly
Bass: Leroy Vinnegar
Drums: Stan Levey

The pairing was irresistible, but for everything the two West Coast icons had in common—searing talent, good looks, and, much to the personal ruin of each, heroin addiction—Chet Baker and Art Pepper didn't really like each other.

If acrimony helped lead to the decision to spin the sextet off into various trios and quartets, it served the record well. The most experimental and intriguing combination is the saxophone trio of Pepper, Leroy Vinnegar, and Stan, with Pepper blowing some breathtaking improvisations in a format ahead of its time. Pete Jolly, whom Stan played with in Shorty Rogers's band, sparkles on the album, and Chet Baker is his usual lyrical self.

DIZZY GILLESPIE, STAN GETZ, AND SONNY STITT, *FOR MUSICIANS ONLY*
(Verve Records, 1956)

Trumpet: Dizzy Gillespie
Tenor saxophone: Stan Getz
Alto saxophone: Sonny Stitt
Piano: John Lewis
Guitar: Herb Ellis
Bass: Ray Brown
Drums: Stan Levey

If cult jazz can be defined as obscure music kept alive by loyal—even fanatical—adherents spanning multiple generations across vast geography, *For Musicians Only* certainly qualifies. Players all over the world continue to grapple with the impossible tempos and sheer physicality of this recording, which is collected globally and hardly ever out of print.

For Musicians Only is an electrifying example of a spontaneous "blowing session." Music without a net can certainly fall flat, but if the chemistry is right, the spontaneous magic unique to jazz can be thrilling. Producer Norman Granz, who always "wanted blood" on his projects, played this one beautifully: What better way to raise the tension and get a little revenge on Stan than by hiring the very guy who sent him to prison? Neither Stan nor Stitt knew the other would be there until the session started.

He started in with the gibberish "*Ahbububu . . . man, you know it wasn't me, man! It was the other guy!*"
I looked him right in the eye and said, almost quietly, "Just shut the fuck up." I'm sorry, am I cursing on your tape? I said, "Just shut up and play your horn." But you know, I

owed the guy, even though he was a fink. I just didn't tell him that.

I went home and told Angela, "You won't believe who I played with on this job." But I really like that record. You could call it a favorite of mine.

The reunion of Stan, Dizzy, and Ray Brown brought back memories of the first trip to California. These cats were heroes to John Lewis, the pianist on the date. As an awestruck teenager in Albuquerque a decade earlier, Lewis had listened, transfixed, to live radio broadcasts from Billy Berg's.

As for Stitt, the talented saxophonist was about as close to Bird as you could get. Not surprisingly though, Stan was unimpressed: "Sonny Stitt, to me, was just a clone of Parker droning out chorus after chorus of licks and more licks . . . I liked him better on tenor, believe it or not." Stan's criticism aside, Stitt's ability to "play his ass off" is manifest on this record.

Some of Granz's productions were criticized as formulaic and hyper-emotive. *For Musicians Only*, however, is an authentically spontaneous, highly charged jam session guaranteed to put listeners back on their tailbones. Stan Getz never played hotter, and Levey steps back into the ring with knockout punches and a rhythmic drive that conjures up the bruising, competitive jam sessions of Kansas City and Harlem. For sheer, blistering energy and freewheeling improvisation, this sets the bar. Ignore the title, crank up the volume, and hang on.

BEN WEBSTER QUINTET, *SOULVILLE*
(Verve Records, 1957)

Tenor saxophone: Ben Webster
Piano: Oscar Peterson
Guitar: Herb Ellis
Bass: Ray Brown
Drums: Stan Levey

Ben Webster was known as "The Brute" among women who experienced his sometimes violent temper. Nevertheless, his music had a devastatingly romantic sound that became a prescription for passion for the *Playboy* generation. Popular even today, *Soulville*'s staying power is attributable to many qualities, including its reputation as a go-to album for amorous evenings of wine and candlelight. Bluesy, breathy, grinding, and slow, Webster's tough but tender evocations continue to captivate women and men everywhere, including the bedroom.

After a couple of sultry blues numbers, the album moves into the gorgeous ballads for which it's famous. Throughout, Stan plays his role as the quintessential timekeeper, holding back in typical fashion to help maximize the potency of Webster's phrasing and emotional range. "It was a pleasure to hear Stan Levey in there," Webster told jazz critic Nat Hentoff. "He's improved a lot since I heard him on [Fifty-Second Street] years ago. It takes time to learn to play the instrument to the point where everyone, including you, is relaxed. Stan's gotten to that point."

Like Miles Davis's *Kind of Blue*, *Soulville* represents the consummate jazz album: a timeless classic and one of the most iconic and enduring records in Stan's discography. Modern reissues include several outtakes at the end that feature Webster on piano—interesting perhaps to historians, but out of sorts with the lusty mood of the core material.

STAN GETZ AND GERRY MULLIGAN,
GETZ MEETS MULLIGAN IN HI-FI
(Verve Records, 1957)

Tenor and baritone saxophone: Stan Getz and Gerry Mulligan
Piano: Lou Levy
Bass: Ray Brown
Drums: Stan Levey

With Ray Brown by his side, Stan could play as quietly as he wanted and still deliver the perfect time and tasteful ideas that artists like these expected from him. This revealing album opens with the sneaky surprise of Gerry Mulligan on tenor and Stan Getz on baritone. The cats have swapped horns! It was Mulligan's idea, but good old Norman Granz deserves credit for encouraging that type of thing. Half the tracks on the original album are rendered through this bewitching re-versal, which sounds like two brothers trying on each other's souls. A wave ensues when they switch back to their normal horns, and the effect is a refreshed appreciation for these ster-ling axes. It's surprising that the album isn't more celebrated for the experiment: a gimmick to some, perhaps, but a daring move undertaken in the spirit of jazz risk and improvisation.

Not surprisingly, it's on the Charlie Parker tune "Scrapple from the Apple" that Stan gets assertive. But as formidable as the rhythm section is, this record is all about the reeds.

MAX ROACH AND STAN LEVEY WITH
HOWARD RUMSEY'S LIGHTHOUSE ALL-STARS,
DRUMMIN' THE BLUES
(Liberty Records, 1957)

Tenor saxophone: Bob Cooper and Bill Perkins
Trombone: Frank Rosolino
Trumpet: Conte Candoli
Piano: Dick Shreve
Bass: Howard Rumsey
Drums: Max Roach and Stan Levey

When Howard Rumsey transitioned from Max Roach to Stan Levey at the Lighthouse, inevitable comparisons arose from the musicians on the bandstand and the fans in the audience.

"Stan was a very simple, basic drummer," said saxophonist Bud Shank, "as opposed to Max, who was complex. But they both achieved the same purpose. They swung like hell."

Drummer Don Lamond offered his take: "I loved Max. He was marvelous. But he could sometimes get a little erratic for my tastes. Stan just flows. He's smooth."

The two drummers were the biggest stars in the Lighthouse stable. Rumsey played off of their friendship with an album that eschews the "battle" formula and instead invites listeners to compare and contrast on alternating tunes between the two pals and bebop pioneers. Rumsey commented on their camaraderie in the liner notes: "Ever since they first met on New York's famous Fifty-Second Street, Max Roach and Stan Levey have felt intuitively that each was the other's personal preference."

This record is considered highly collectible in Japan.

STAN LEVEY QUINTET, *STAN LEVEY QUINTET*
(Mode Records, 1957)

Tenor saxophone: Richie Kamuca
Trumpet: Conte Candoli
Piano: Lou Levy
Bass: Monty Budwig
Drums: Stan Levey

Tight as a trampoline, Stan's quintet flows through a set packed with ideas and killer moments. Richie Kamuca is the big contributor, penning two originals and all the arrangements, but pianist Lou Levy steals the show with some mind-bending solos. Lou Levy came out of Chicago and played in many of the same bands as Stan, including those of Woody Herman, Peggy Lee, Ella Fitzgerald, and Stan Getz. This record finds him in top form, blending speedy runs with soulful, depth-plumbing phrases that seem to dig into the very guts of the piano. The album peaks on "Lover Come Back to Me," a ballad-turned-burner that climaxes with an effervescent solo from Stan.

BILL HARRIS, *BILL HARRIS AND FRIENDS*
(Fantasy Records, 1957)

Trombone: Bill Harris
Tenor saxophone: Ben Webster
Piano: Jimmy Rowels
Bass: Red Mitchell
Drums: Stan Levey

A stellar gem of casual jazz from a forgotten artist. Ben Webster fans will revel in the pairing with Bill Harris, a stylist of self-taught individualism who weaves his animated trombone around Webster's succulent sax. Stan called his old Philly gasman and Woody Herman bandmate "a trombone genius." Few who hear this will disagree.

HAMPTON HAWES, *THE SERMON*
(Contemporary Records, 1958)

Piano: Hampton Hawes
Bass: Leroy Vinnegar
Drums: Stan Levey

Stan's interracial experience was highly unusual for a man of his time. From his days working out at the Spring Garden Gym to his nights sharing beds with Bird and Miles Davis in Harlem, Stan had always, as Oscar Smith said, "sort of passed for black." Now, in the thick of "white coast" cool, Hampton Hawes was calling on the Jewish drummer to help interpret the sacred Christian music of the black church.

The album was deeply personal for Hawes. His father was minister of the Westminster Presbyterian Church in Watts, and Hawes had been steeped in gospel, hymns, and spirituals since birth. If ever there was a time that he needed to draw from the spiritual well, it was now; a few days after this record date, Hawes would face a judge for sentencing on a heroin charge.

Stan admired Hawes as a player but also as a "stand-up guy"—the opposite of Sonny Stitt. Hawes's arrest was the result of an undercover sting set up by Harry Anslinger's FBN. By refusing to cooperate or inform, Hawes was potentially looking at hard time. In the liner notes for *The Sermon*, Mike Davis wrote: "Hamp refused the offer of 'freedom in exchange for cooperation.' Not because of any sense of *omerta* [the criminal code of silence], but because he believed that to accept the deal would be like taking thirty pieces of silver to administer a Judas kiss."

After completing *The Sermon*, Hawes went before the judge, who sentenced him to a devastating ten years in federal prison.

The Sermon offers choice samplings of Stan's creative brushwork. He swishes the snare in alternating whispers and shouts, with restrained and respectful accents that move to the front of the aisle on the closing blues, where Stan gives testimony in one of his most inspired accompaniments on record.

Hawes was remanded to Fort Worth, the same prison where Stan served time. While Hawes was imprisoned, *The Sermon* sat on the shelf, unreleased.

FRANK ROSOLINO, *FREE FOR ALL*
(Specialty Records, 1958)

Trombone: Frank Rosolino
Tenor saxophone: Harold Land
Piano: Victor Feldman
Bass: Leroy Vinnegar
Drums: Stan Levey

One of the first hard bop albums recorded on the West Coast, *Free For All* was a provocative, well-rounded session with ingenious arrangements, inspired improvisations, and tight glue. Ideas abound, and it swings from start to finish. But for some reason, Specialty Records decided not to release it.

"I feel it's the best album I have ever recorded," a frustrated Rosolino wrote to the company. "Everyone who was on the date feels the same. I've played the dub for numerous musicians and they all think it's just great."

Stan concurred. Earlier in the year, he told *Downbeat* magazine, "Harold Land I just love . . . I'm waiting for Harold to really become well-known throughout the country as one of the best tenor players to blow a horn. And I don't think that will be too long now."

Buried with the album was an original tune by Stan, a bebop number titled "Chrisdee" (a combination of his son Chris's name with little David's nickname, "Dee-dee") into which Stan wrote a rare solo for Leroy Vinnegar, the rhythmically reliable bassist who perfected the "walking" style and contributed his impeccable playing to dozens of classic West Coast sessions. Hailing from the jazz sleeper town of Indianapolis, Vinnegar also appeared on seminal albums like Van Morrison's *Saint Dominic's Preview* and Eddie Harris and Les McCann's *Swiss Movement*, widely recognized for the blockbuster number "Compared to What."

Free For All should have been one of Rosolino's finest albums. His producer, David Axelrod, remarked, "It was a great disappointment to us both that the record, for reasons we never understood, wasn't released."

The album would eventually be released, but not until many years after the unspeakable tragedy that led to Rosolino's horrific death.

VICTOR FELDMAN, *THE ARRIVAL OF VICTOR FELDMAN*
(Contemporary Records, 1958)

Vibraphone and piano: Victor Feldman
Bass: Scott LaFaro
Drums: Stan Levey

"Dad's stuff with Victor Feldman has such an extreme, high-velocity groove that it's almost cult jazz. It's hard to imagine anything that swings harder."

—David Levey

Charlie Watts purchased this album immediately after its arrival in the U.K. Copies were snatched up all over Feldman's native England, where the brilliant multi-instrumentalist first appeared on the scene as a child prodigy drummer. Feldman went on to master the piano and vibraphone, and he plays both on this modern classic.

"Being English of my generation," Watts said, "we were extremely proud of Victor Feldman, who moved to Hollywood and made it, which was unheard of for an Englishman at the time. And Stan . . . along with a fantastic bass player named Scott LaFaro, played on *The Arrival of Victor Feldman*. A very famous album. A trio. I didn't know until much later that Stan's wife, Angela, who's just as interesting as Stan, took the picture on the cover with the three of them on a boat."

Nobody would argue with Watts's assessment of LaFaro. The young virtuoso's performance on this album, LaFaro's breakout appearance on record, must have been downright frightening to his peers. LaFaro and Feldman arrived in Stan's orbit at roughly the same time, with Feldman joining the All-Stars and LaFaro sitting in frequently. The three had a cerebral chemistry that swirls through compositions by Ellington,

Chopin, and some Feldman originals.

Stan also brought in a Dizzy Gillespie tune that really spiced things up. "Bebop" was, according to Feldman, "faster than I've ever recorded." Lou Brown, who was present in the studio, said, "Victor had a tempo in mind. Stan said, 'Come on, man, you can do it faster than that.' Victor didn't really want to. But Stan forced him to play at that tempo." Stan plays "Bebop" like he owns it, with a restrained intensity that's almost unbearable. Stan once called *The Arrival* "the best thing I ever played on."

LaFaro later joined pianist Bill Evans and drummer Paul Motion in an ensemble that revolutionized the piano trio. *The Arrival* is recognized as a foreshadowing of this celebrated group and their key contributions to the development of jazz. Feldman went on to work with many of the greats, including Miles Davis. In the 1970s, he remained one of the most in-demand musicians on the coast, and a key contributor on crossover recordings by Frank Zappa, Joni Mitchell, Tom Waits, and Steely Dan.

EPILOGUE

HARRY ANSLINGER served under four presidents for a total of thirty-two years as narcotics commissioner. He had more influence on American drug policy in the twentieth century than any other individual, and remains a controversial and often ridiculed figure even today. If racial prejudice and square musical taste contributed to Anslinger's acrimony toward jazz musicians, so too did a sober realization that others would emulate them. In 1964, he wrote a book called *The Protectors* in which he quoted Chet Baker:

> "My arms have been punctured more than thirty thousand times to get morphine and heroin into my veins," Baker ruminated. "Why? Hadn't Charlie Parker, one of the greatest jazz talents America has ever produced, been an addict? Couldn't I too, be a genius with the intravenous aid of narcotics? If there is a shortcut to complete musical fulfillment, drugs don't provide it. They're a shortcut to the nuthouse and the grave."

In *The Protectors*, Anslinger also wrote:

Jazz entertainers are neither fish nor fowl. They do not get the million-dollar protection Hollywood and Broadway can afford for their stars who have become addicted—and there are many more than will ever be revealed. Perhaps this is because jazz, once considered

a decadent kind of music, has only token respectability.
Jazz grew up next door to crime, so to speak. Clubs
of dubious reputation were, for a long time, the only
places where it could be heard. But the times bring
changes, and as Billie Holiday was a victim of time
and change, so too was Charlie Parker, a man whose
music, like Billie's, is still widely imitated. Most musicians credit Parker among others as spearheading what
is called modern jazz.

Harry Anslinger died in 1975 at the age of eighty-three.
Eleven years later, President Ronald Reagan gave Anslinger his
due in a speech: "The first federal law enforcement adminis-
trator to recognize the signs of a national criminal syndication
and sound the alarm was Harry J. Anslinger."

After working with Stan for Bethlehem and with Peggy Lee,
bassist **MAX BENNETT** became the most seamless crossover artist in the business. Equally adept on both upright and
electric, Bennett found himself flourishing with younger musicians, playing on classic records like Frank Zappa's *Hot Rats*,
Cat Stevens's "Peace Train," and other discs by artists as varied
as Diana Ross and Arlo Guthrie. Joni Mitchell was especially
fond of Bennett's work; he played on several of her best albums,
including *Court and Spark* and *The Hissing of Summer Lawns*.

"What people like Frank and Joni found out was that the
jazz musicians were the most versatile," said Bennett. "They
all read well and were very adaptable to different kinds of music. They could do rock, jazz, or anything in between. The
country boys couldn't quite cut it."

Bennett was also a founding member of what turned out

to be the last great Lighthouse band, an outfit that came to be known as Tom Scott and the L.A. Express.

"It was about 1972," Bennett recalled. "I got a call from Tom Scott, saying, 'Could you help me out? I'm down at the Lighthouse.' I said, 'Well, can I play Fender?' And he said, 'Sure.' I went down and as we played one of my originals, a light bulb went on. It was Tom, Joe Sample, me, and pretty soon, John Guerin and Larry Carlton. Joni Mitchell flipped out over the band, and we went on tour with her. Five grand a week! In the '70s? C'mon! Joni was a great chick. One of the best people I ever worked for in my life. She was wonderful to play with and hang out with. Very intellectual and very down-home."

Well into his eighties, Max Bennett is still playing. His current band, Private Reserve, is heavy on the jazz.

"Not much money around here, but we do our best," he said. "I like rock and roll . . . to a point. Some rock bands, like Led Zeppelin—now that's a great band, period. But I wouldn't last long in one of the regular rock and roll bands because I would get starved harmonically. Not enough room for self-expression. The audience wants to hear the same stuff every night. And, matter of fact, they get pissed if you don't play it!

"Stan was a great guy. I lived next door to him and Angela near the beach, and she kind of took me under her wing—feeding me dinner. And Stan helped get me into Kenton's band. He got busted, but he was Mr. Straight Arrow after that. My wife and I went to his funeral, and we really miss him."

In August 2014, at Los Angeles Local 47 of the Musicians Union, just up the street from **BILLY BERG'S** old location on

Vine Street, the Los Angeles Jazz Institute hosted a concert commemorating the introduction of bebop to California. John Fadis played the Dizzy role, while Charles McPherson subbed for Charlie Parker. Charlie Shoemake honored Milt Jackson, while Edwin Livingston channeled Ray Brown. Tom Ranier sat in Al Haig's chair, and drummer Paul Kreibich chased the furious tempos set by Stan Levey. Five hundred people packed the hall to hear the once-controversial music that now informs virtually all American music made since. Charlie Shoemake commented that bebop was "the hardest stuff that anybody would ever have to play as far as technical demands. That's about as high as the human quality can manage."

Shoemake's wife, Sandi, remembered a dinner date she and Charlie had with Stan and Angela on Halloween. "Some trick-or-treaters came knocking, and here comes this big, menacing guy to the door and he's just the essence of sweetness and nice with these little kiddos: 'Now, don't eat too much of these, it's bad for your toothies.'"

The Lighthouse's cousin on the East Coast, **BIRDLAND**, closed in 1965, only to reopen twenty-one years later on the Upper West Side. Now back in Midtown, Birdland continues to feature the biggest names in jazz.

CONTE CANDOLI stayed on the West Coast, blowing his way through the '60s with small bands and session work. In what turned out to be impeccable timing, considering the grim state of jazz in the '70s, Candoli took a steady gig with *The Tonight Show* Band in 1972 and held the job for twenty years. Candoli died of cancer in 2001 at the age of seventy-four.

After his stint with the Lighthouse All-Stars, **SONNY CLARK** moved to New York City and became a sought-after sideman. He recorded many classic sides for Blue Note Records, where, for a short time at least, he held the piano chair as the quintessential hard bop pianist, known less for his solos than his rhythmically inventive accompaniment. As a leader, the albums he put out were consistently excellent and, along with his sideman dates, highly prized by aficionados. Stan was devastated when he got word of Sonny's death from a heroin overdose in 1963. The pianist was only thirty-one years old.

After admonishing Stan and Dexter Gordon for using heroin, **MILES DAVIS** himself became an addict. After a rapid decline, Davis spared himself the cement cure by checking himself into his father's farmhouse in Missouri. Miles Sr. stood by while his son suffered through withdrawal and finally emerged a free man, poised to become the vanguard of jazz for the next four decades.

He and Stan remained friends, getting together occasionally at Davis's estate in Malibu when he was in California. Davis went through constant changes in sound and style, yet Stan insisted that he was exactly the same guy he was when they roomed together in the '40s. Miles Davis died in 1991 at age sixty-five.

Stan once told an interviewer in Liverpool that **VICTOR FELDMAN** was "one of the greatest things you people ever sent over here—one of greatest imports that ever happened."

"Victor and Marilyn were two of our best friends," said Angela. "We stood up for them at their wedding. We had dinners together . . . Marilyn and I played tennis together. When they told me she had died . . . at her age . . . oh, I'm still not over it. At the funeral, I put my arms around Vic and he felt like a little tiny bird and he was shaking like a leaf, and it was shortly after that he died, and it was as close as you can get to dying of a broken heart, I think."

Feldman died of a heart attack in 1987 at age fifty-three.

ERROLL GARNER never learned to read music, but he practiced religiously and earned an international reputation as the most distinctive pianist of his time. His powerful swing and ornate arpeggios won him popular appeal and even a little wealth. In 1955, he recorded *Concert by the Sea,* one of the best-selling jazz albums ever. Garner's original composition "Misty" became a standard that was used to chilling effect in Clint Eastwood's psychotic thriller *Play Misty for Me.* Garner died in 1977.

Stan and Angela were on hand to welcome **STAN GETZ** when he moved to California.

"Donte's was a good club on Lankershim Boulevard in North Hollywood," Angela remembered. "Getz had just come in from New York. I was on the sidewalk waiting for Stan, and I looked across the street and Getz steps out of a cab. I looked at him and I said, 'Stanley! You cannot dress like that out here!' It was hot and he was wearing a blue serge suit. 'You look like a businessman!'"

Getz's sea breeze of a sound came to epitomize West Coast jazz, even though his time on the scene was relatively brief. Later, his bossa nova records made him wealthy and world-famous.

Getz created a majestic body of work, and his sound alone

became one of the great joys of jazz. But his life outside of music was driven largely by opiate addiction, and was consequently filled with sadness, heartbreak, and eventually, cancer. Getz died in 1991 at age sixty-four while sitting in his wheelchair, looking out at the Pacific Ocean.

"We had a good time together," said Stan. "He was a great player and I really miss him."

DIZZY GILLESPIE became an American icon at home and abroad. The state department even hired him to take jazz around the world as an official cultural ambassador of the United States of America. After inventing bebop, he contributed to the development of Afro-Cuban jazz and continued to write original compositions that became standards. His trumpet supremacy was unquestioned and his personality, positive attitude, and good humor endeared him to the masses. He was a teacher, a role model, and an alter ego to Charlie Parker.

"I have been married all my life," Gillespie said. "My wife is very religious, and that has prevented me from doing things that were detrimental to me. I needed someone who was in my corner. My wife gave me that strength, like an anchor . . . My tastes don't run that high . . . I am a millionaire because there are very few things I wanted and was unable to get. The simple reason for that is I don't want too much . . . I try to eat the proper foods, I stay free from alcohol and drugs, and I live like a married man should, which is also very important."

Gillespie achieved mass popularity without compromising his art. In the 1970s, his pianist, Mike Longo, claimed that Gillespie had musical secrets that some of the greatest musicians still did not understand or appreciate.

Gillespie lived a complete life, replete with awards and recognition, and died in 1993 at age seventy-five.

"By all standards," Stan said, " he was a man."

After playing on *This Time the Drum's On Me*, **DEXTER GORDON** returned to prison on another heroin charge and spent the rest of the 1950s behind bars. In the 1960s, he recorded a string of records for Blue Note before moving to Europe. Gordon staged another comeback in the '80s, receiving an Academy Award nomination for his leading role in the 1986 film *Round Midnight*, and solidifying himself as one of the boss tenors in jazz history. In 1990, he fell ill in Philadelphia and was admitted to Thomas Jefferson Hospital, where Chris Levey was working rotations as a third-year medical student in his father's hometown.

"One morning, I'm reviewing the charts and I see the name 'Dexter Gordon,'" said Chris. "No way! I wasn't on his service, but I made a point to drop in and talk to him. He had renal failure and your mind gets a little groggy, but when I told him who I was, he said, 'Yeah man! Stan! Yeah, yeah!' He wasn't real coherent, but he was certainly pleasant."

Gordon never left Thomas Jefferson. He died there a few weeks later at age sixty-seven.

AL HAIG, Stan's white counterpart with Bird and Diz, faded from the jazz scene not long after the bebop revolution. In 1958, the young vibraphonist Charlie Shoemake invoked the name of Al Haig after summoning the nerve to approach Stan at the Lighthouse. Shoemake never forgot Stan's response.

"I said, 'Hey, Stan, I have a recording of you with Stan Getz from 1949. Al Haig is one of my heroes.'

"'Well, you better get another one,' Stan deadpanned."

In the 1970s, Haig reemerged to make some obscure but critically acclaimed albums for small record labels, and he enjoyed some success in Europe and Japan before dying from a heart attack in 1982. During his long disappearance, Haig was accused of murdering his wife. He was acquitted in 1969, but many, including Stan, figured him for guilty.

> Al Haig was from Nutley, New Jersey, and he looked like a little bank teller. Him I never figured out. Later on he killed his wife. Yeah! Mr. Milquetoast. Strangled his wife. Killed her. And got off! Somehow he got off. Somebody got him off, but everybody knows he did it.

While serving his ten-year prison term, HAMPTON HAWES filed a long-shot application for executive clemency. In 1963, five years into his sentence and to the amazement of his fellow prisoners, President John F. Kennedy granted Hawes a pardon. Though undocumented, one can't help but wonder if this clemency didn't help endear Stan to JFK.

After some fits and starts, Hawes's career languished and he died of a stroke in 1977 at age forty-eight. Ten years after his death, and a full twenty-nine years after it was made, *The Sermon* was finally released to great critical acclaim.

WOODY HERMAN had one of the few big bands to survive and flourish in the decades beyond the swing era. Beloved by his musicians, Herman credited his success, which did not come without his share of suffering, to his Catholic faith and lifelong marriage.

In the 1960s, his manager gambled away the money set

aside for taxes. Herman spent the next two decades exhausting himself in servitude to the IRS. He was evicted from his home while on his deathbed before Lenny Garment swooped in and stopped the IRS from making the sale. In 1987, Herman died penniless but at peace with his life and legacy. He took with him to his grave the scar on his leg from a gangster's bullet—a memento from another era.

RICHIE KAMUCA finished out the 1950s working with Shelly Manne before moving back East for ten years, where he worked with artists like Gerry Mulligan and Roy Eldridge. In 1972, he returned to the West Coast, where he recorded three acclaimed albums for the Concord label before developing cancer.

"When cats got sick like Richie, dad was a center of solace," said David Levey. "He was the guy wheeling Richie to the car, driving him to the beach, and sitting him on the sand where he liked to look out and watch the birds. Dad was the same way later on with Buddy Rich, and I think it had something to do with the fact that he always wanted to be a doctor, but had a bit of a heavy heart knowing he could've never gotten there with his upbringing and lack of education and advantage."

Kamuca died in Los Angeles, one day before his forty-seventh birthday.

While still touring in 1977, **STAN KENTON** took a fall in Pennsylvania and fractured his skull. He never fully recovered, and died of a stroke two years later at age sixty-seven. Like his fellow Californians and Wall of Sounders the Grateful Dead, Kenton was panned by critics but beloved by fanatical legions who didn't mind a little human mediocrity mixed with astonishing playing, killer arrangements, and magical moments. One such fan was the comedian Mort Sahl, a Kenton aficionado who alluded to Kenton's critics as "dilettantes."

Like Harry Anslinger, Kenton fell fodder to ridicule in pop culture as an example of the proverbial square—a pale-face of jazz. Nevertheless, his experimentalism, his best works, and the collective contributions of the musicians who passed through his band are all still admired by a West Coast cult of Hollywood composers, Deadheads, and Zappaphiles who appreciate loud, mind-blowing music.

I'm so sorry his life ended the way it did because he had this alcohol problem that I wasn't really aware of. I never saw him drink. And he died relatively broke.

He took a chance on me: "Are you okay?" "Yeah, I'm okay." That's a great guy. And he was a very honest guy. He'd give you his word on something—you could take it to the bank. Kenton was about forty when we were in the band and we were all in our mid-twenties, so he was something of a father figure, just a great guy, and we all miss him.

In Stan's estimation, **ROCCO SCOTT LAFARO** was the most inspiring bassist of his generation. The young innovator woodshedded for eight hours a day and transformed the bass into an instrument that flowed like a piano and a conversed like a saxophone.

After playing the Newport Jazz Festival with Stan Getz in July 1961, LaFaro visited his hometown of Geneva, New York, where a late-night drive with a high school buddy turned to tragedy when the two young men crashed into a tree, killing them both. LaFaro was only twenty-five years old.

Immortalized mainly through his work with Bill Evans, LaFaro's fluidity and interplay have been studied by bassists ever since, and his influence is heard in the work of prodigies like Stanley Clarke.

"Scotty was a genius," said Stan. "Angela loved him. Broke our hearts. What a loss when that kid died, my God."

PEGGY LEE and **ELLA FITZGERALD** both became living legends, aging into their golden years filled with recognition but also plagued with ill health. Fitzgerald lost her eyesight and had to have both legs amputated below the knees. Lee, too, ended up in a wheelchair, and both died from complications of diabetes and heart trouble, Fitzgerald in 1996 at age seventy-nine, and Lee in 2002 at age eighty-one. Both left legacies and appeal that seem destined to last for generations. Fitzgerald was honored with her own postage stamp, and Lee with a hybrid rose.

ANGELA LEVEY'S self-deprecating description of her current status belies her enviable appearance, active lifestyle, and razor-sharp wit. She is, in her own words, "living and breathing, but completely miserable without Stan."

THE LIGHTHOUSE remains in Hermosa Beach. Visitors to the area will find it anchoring the same Pier Avenue address it did back in the 1950s, when the All-Stars held court five nights a week. Reggae, country, and karaoke now share the bill, but cats still come to blow, and the Sunday jazz brunch is an ongoing tradition.

STEVE LUKATHER and his bandmates in Toto reached the peak of commercial success in the 1980s with mega hits like "Africa" and "Rosanna." Casual fans might be unaware of their collective contributions to the work of other musicians. These include appearances and songwriting credits on over five thousand albums, including Michael Jackson's *Thriller*, which became the best-selling album of all time thanks in no small part to Toto's key contributions.

Lukather has collected five Grammys over the years, and remains one of the few rock musicians versatile enough to play with heavy cats like Miles Davis, Herbie Hancock, and Wayne Shorter. Davis even recorded one of Lukather's songs and played on Toto's *Fahrenheit* album. Stan got a kick out of the fact that his old bebop buddy and roommate was now working with the kid from his garage.

"Stan thought we were knuckleheads," Lukather said. "Runts with long hair. He never thought we'd pull it off. I think he cracked up when he found out we did. But ultimately, I think he's ecstatic that Chris and David never became full-time musicians, but rather went into medicine."

SHELLY MANNE became a paradox of ubiquity and anonymity. His gamut ran from the big bands of Benny Goodman and Stan Kenton to the edgy visions of Ornette Coleman and Tom Waits, and he played on hundreds of movies and television soundtracks. He was everywhere, yet the public hardly knew his name. In 1959, Manne released a series of live albums recorded at the Black Hawk in San Francisco that are still prized by connoisseurs as stellar examples of live jazz for the ages. That same year he opened Shelly's Manne Hole, a top club in Los Angeles for twelve years where Robert Levey worked a stint as a doorman. Shelly died of a heart attack in 1984 at age sixty-four.

OSCAR PETTIFORD moved to Europe in 1958. He died in Copenhagen two years later at the age of thirty-eight—another causality to the hard-living ways of the bebop era.

After trading places with Stan at the Lighthouse, MAX ROACH partnered with trumpet star Clifford Brown to form one of the most highly regarded quintets in jazz history. In 1960, Roach released *We Insist! Max Roach's Freedom Now Suite*, a riveting, avant-garde exploration of the African American struggle for civil rights. Later, Roach landed a job teaching at the University of Massachusetts while continuing to record, perform, and experiment.

Stan recalled seeing Max in the early years of the twenty-first century with a band consisting only of drums, tenor, trumpet, and trombone—an effort that had Stan scratching his head. Max Roach collected a plethora of awards and honorary degrees before outliving Stan by two years, passing away in 2007 at the age of eighty-three.

The fate of FRANK ROSOLINO is unspeakable yet necessary in a biography of Stan Levey, who was one of his closest friends and musical associates. In 1978, Rosolino's ex-wife and mother of his two young sons committed suicide. A few months later, Rosolino, the funniest and most lovable man in jazz, shot both of his sons while they slept, killing nine-year-old Justin and permanently blinding seven-year-old Jason. Frank then turned the gun on himself.

The jazz world, a subculture strong in connections and camaraderie, was devastated. After the initial grief, Rosolino's friends and fellow musicians generally suppressed the memory of him, and even his music.

"Stan was livid," said Angela. "He didn't often show his feelings, but every time it came up, he would express anger. He never softened on it. We both felt negative towards Frank for a long, long, time, until recently, going through all the pictures, I really feel like he snapped and had a mental illness, and it's hard for me to judge somebody like that."

In 1986, eighteen years after it was recorded and eight years after Frank Rosolino's death, *Free For All* was finally released to great critical acclaim. At the time of its release, Stan told his old friend Leonard Feather that Frank had "put into his music much more than he ever achieved out of it."

HOWARD RUMSEY stayed on at the Lighthouse until 1971, when he opened his own club on the Redondo Beach pier called Concerts by the Sea, which he ran until 1985. He considered his time with Stan as the high point in the All-Stars' history, and appreciated the drummer's work ethic as much as his musicianship.

"Stan was an absolute paragon of professionalism," said Rumsey. "Never came late. Never was a disappointment in any way. Really did the job. He had the highest standards of performance of any drummer I've encountered."

One of the key figures of West Coast jazz, Howard Rumsey lived to the age of ninety-nine before passing away in 2015.

After Dizzy Gillespie replaced him with Ray Brown, CURLY RUSSELL found work with Monk, Miles, Dexter, Hawkins,

Art Blakey, and other top artists of the 1950s. By the end of the decade, however, he was playing mostly rhythm and blues and Catskills dates.

Russell left the music business in 1966 and died in Queens twenty years later at age sixty-nine. His snub of Stan was a blip in their friendship and musical camaraderie. "Curly was a good friend of ours in New York," said Angela. "We just liked each other, and he was a very sweet man."

When the writer Jack Kerouac decided to make spoken-word recordings on the West Coast, the Birdland habitué naturally desired jazz accompaniment to his beat. He found the right cat in **ZOOT SIMS,** whose life and music had been overlapping with Stan's since their teenage sojourn with Benny Goodman.

Unlike Stan, though, Sims drank almost as hard as he played—and he played very, very hard. By the 1970s, he had worked so many jobs and made so many records that he was halfway-famous. A sax-playing Muppet was even named after him on the popular television show. When he wasn't blowing, Sims enjoyed digging in the dirt and growing things. He remained an indefatigable player right up to the end, when cancer took him in 1985.

Legend has it that when **SONNY STITT** asked Miles Davis for a raise and was refused, he said, "No money, no Sonny!" and left the band.

Due in part to his betrayal of Stan, Sonny Stitt's own prison sentence for selling narcotics was much shorter than it might have been. Stan was hardly the only one to criticize Stitt as a Parker clone, but many insiders argued that Sonny's style, though similar, was developed independently and not copied.

One can't help but respect Stitt's response to the comparison with Bird, which was to master tenor as well as alto.

Sonny also made commendable changes to his attitude and behavior. Like Stan, he managed to kick the heroin habit and make a good living as a high-level and hard-working jazz musician in the '50s and '60s. He toured and recorded mainly as a freelancer, but also had a celebrated partnership with Gene Ammons.

"I've made my mistakes," Stitt told Les Tomkins in 1965. "I ain't going to say that I wasn't wrong about a lot of things in my life. But I did learn to try to make myself more respectable in jazz, and not act like an idiot. This is a great profession we have, and it should be respected highly. . . . All musicians are not perverts, dope fiends, or bad-acting characters, and I hope the people learn to understand that everyone in this world is human, and there will be mistakes that they will make. But when the man or woman that makes the mistake corrects it—give him credit. Because it may be hard for him to change himself, to conform to society's ways of living. I try to be a good man, and to lead a Christian life to the best of my ability. And I just want people to learn that jazz is a wonderful thing."

With his terrific playing, Stitt certainly did his part in making jazz a wonderful thing. He died of a heart attack in 1982 at the age of fifty-eight.

ART TATUM moved to the West Coast shortly after his record date with Stan, and he was one of the curious musicians who came to Billy Berg's to hear the beboppers. He continued to play and record prolifically, both as a solo artist and in the piano trio format. Tatum was known to drink a case of Pabst Blue Ribbon and two quarts of whiskey a day—a habit that led to diabetes and early death from uremia at age forty-six.

Some critics and musicians considered Tatum's music too orchestral for jazz, but most simply marveled at his inimitable outpourings. Horowitz, Rubinstein, Rachmaninoff, Gershwin, and other piano greats eulogized him as a genius. Teddy Wilson said, "Maybe this will explain Art Tatum. If you put a piano in a room . . . then you get all the finest jazz pianists in the world and let them play in the presence of Art Tatum. Then let Art Tatum play . . . everyone there will sound like an amateur."

SHIRLEY VAN DYKE landed bit parts in various films, including *Around the World in Eighty Days*, before joining the U.S. Postal Service, starting out as a mail carrier and eventually co-founding their drug and alcohol recovery program. "She helped a lot of people," said her son, Robert. The program was so successful, it earned Van Dyke an award from President Ronald Reagan.

Van Dyke put in twenty years with the Postal Service, but she never got a chance to enjoy retirement, passing away in 1989 at age sixty-four. "Mom was always looking for a guy to make her legit," said Robert. "It took me many years to realize how sick she was. Dad and Angela never said one bad thing about her."

Decades of workmanlike dedication paid off for **LEROY VIN-NEGAR** in the 1980s, when he moved to Portland, Oregon, and became the elder statesman of jazz there before passing away from a heart attack in 1999 at the age of seventy-one. In 2002, Portland State University established the Leroy Vinnegar Jazz Institute, dedicated to "letting knowledge serve the city through programs and partnerships in jazz education and jazz history, public outreach, and service to the artistic community."

When **CHARLIE WATTS** visited the Leveys in 2003, Stan was struggling with throat cancer. A year later, Watts received the same diagnosis, and experienced many of the same symptoms. The Englishman took to calling his old idol from all corners of the world for advice and encouragement. "Dad would tell him what to expect and how to cope, and he gave Charlie some hope," said David Levey. "Charlie was thankful for their relationship in many different ways."

Watts's cancer has since gone into remission and the drummer is still going strong, supported by his wife, Shirley, whom he married in 1964 before the Rolling Stones became famous. A living link between jazz and rock and roll, Watts has remained a tireless jazz ambassador, recording big band and small group albums, sitting in at tiny clubs, and even penning a children's book about Charlie Parker, *Ode to a Highflying Bird*. His reverence for the music and awareness of its history has helped bring generations of rock fans into the jazz camp, and Watts's legacy as a jazz drummer is as solid as a rolling stone.

ACKNOWLEDGMENTS

Stan was emphatically grateful to Charlie Watts for entering his life in his final years and for participating in his biography.

Special thanks go to Angela Levey, whose enduring love for her husband was hugely inspiring, and who also worked hard on this book and gave much, even when it wasn't easy.

And special thanks also to Robert Levey, who gave so generously of his time and efforts, especially in the areas of boxing research and Levey family history. Blessings, Bob!

Arthur Pritz, Sid Davis, Richard Clayman, Burt Korall, Philip Abbott, Alex Cline, Leonard Feather, and Steve Vole all interviewed Stan over a period of fifteen years, helping to preserve his stories and quotes.

Steven Harris, jazz historian and author of the excellent book *The Kenton Kronicles*, helped provide material that—were it not for him—would have evaporated with the mists of time.

Jazz journalist Steven Cerra graciously shared his vivid personal anecdotes of Stan during the Lighthouse era.

Miriam Graham went above and beyond as an editor. She's a great friend, musician, and ranger.

Monica Schreiber's discernment and creativity helped make this a better book. John and Helga Hayde helped with ideas and enthusiasm. The author's lovely wife, Julie, was uncompromising in her support.

Caley Gredig helped tremendously with research and genealogy. She was the portal to other helpful researchers like Jill Rawnsley of the Philadelphia City Archives, Peggy Hatfield of the *Courier* and *Enquirer* Archives, Darlene Layton of the Pennsylvania Department of Health, Brenda Galloway-Wright of Temple University Archives, and Heather Perez of the Atlantic City Library. Thanks, Caley!

On the boxing front, we have several fine men to thank. Henry Hascup's dedication to boxing history is appreciated far and wide. He's the "Uncrowned King of Sports Information." Mike DeLisa, author of the classic Jimmy Braddock biography *The Cinderella Man*, graciously assisted, as did the writer John DiSanto and IBRO director Dan Cuoco. Two fine sons of Philadelphia, George Silvano and Chuck Hasson, donated material and shared their expertise on Philly boxing. Like Dizzy Gillespie, these gentlemen gave freely of their knowledge, and we consider them great flame-keepers and all-around great guys

And speaking of fine sons of Philly, special thanks to Wallace Roney—trumpet master, former boxer, and Miles Davis protégé who's assistance on this project was the epitome of graciousness.

SOURCES

BOOKS

Anslinger, Harry J., and Dennis Gregory. *The Protectors: The Heroic Story of the Narcotics Agents, Citizens, and Officials in Their Unending, Unsung Battles Against Organized Crime in America and Abroad*. Farrar and Straus, 1964.

Anslinger, Harry J., and Will Oursler. *The Murderers: The Shocking Story of the Narcotic Gangs*. Farrar, Straus and Cudahy Company, 1961.

Balliett, Whitney. *American Musicians: 56 Portraits in Jazz*. Oxford University Press, 1986.

Britt, Stan. *Dexter Gordon: A Musical Biography*. Da Capo Press, 1989.

Callis, Tracy, Chuck Hasson, and Mike DeLisa. *Philadelphia's Boxing Heritage 1876–1976*. Arcadia Publishing, 2002.

Chilton, John. *The Song of the Hawk: The Life and Recordings of Coleman Hawkins*. University of Michigan Press, 1990.

Crow, Bill. *Jazz Anecdotes: Second Time Around*. Oxford University Press, 2005.

Davis, Miles, and Quincy Troupe. *Miles: The Autobiography*. Simon and Schuster, 1989.

DeVeaux, Scott. *The Birth of Bebop: A Social and Musical History*. University of California Press, 1997.

Driggs, Frank, and Chuck Haddix. *Kansas City Jazz: From Ragtime to Bebop—A History*. Oxford University Press, 2005.

Ellison, Ralph, and Robert O'Meally (ed.). *Living with Music: Ralph Ellison's Jazz Writings*. Modern Library, 2002.

English, T. J. *Havana Nocturne: How the Mob Owned Cuba . . . and Then Lost It to the Revolution*. William Morrow, 2007.

Fox, Stephen. *Blood and Power: Organized Crime in Twentieth-Century America*. Penguin, 1989.

Friedman, Robert I. *Red Mafiya: How the Russian Mob Has Invaded America*. Little, Brown and Company, 2000.

Garment, Leonard. *Crazy Rhythm: From Brooklyn and Jazz to Nixon's White House, Watergate, and Beyond*. Da Capo Press, 1997.

Gibbs, Terry, and Cary Ginell. *Good Vibes: A Life in Jazz*. Scarecrow Press, 2003.

Harris, Steven D. *The Kenton Kronicles: A Biography of Modern America's Man of Music, Stan Kenton.* Dynaflow Publications, 2000.

Hayde, Frank. *The Mafia and the Machine: The Story of the Kansas City Mob.* Barricade Books, 2007.

Giddins, Gary. *Celebrating Bird: The Triumph of Charlie Parker.* University of Minnesota Press, 1987.

Giddins, Gary, and Scott DeVeaux. *Jazz.* W. W. Norton & Company, 2009

Gillespie, Dizzy, and Al Fraser. *To Be or Not . . . to Bop.* Doubleday, 1979.

Gioia, Ted. *West Coast Jazz: Modern Jazz in California 1945–1960.* Oxford University Press. 1992.

Gitler, Ira. *The Masters of Bebop: A Listener's Guide.* Da Capo Press, 1966.

Greenspan, Alan. *The Age of Turbulence: Adventures in a New World.* Penguin Press, 2007.

Haddix, Chuck. *Bird: The Life and Music of Charlie Parker.* University of Illinois Press, 2013.

Hawes, Hampton, and Don Asher. *Raise Up Off Me: A Portrait of Hampton Hawes.* DaCapo, 1972.

Korall, Burt. *Drummin' Men: The Heartbeat of Jazz: The Swing Years.* Schirmer Books, 1990.

———. *Drummin' Men: The Heartbeat of Jazz: The Swing Years.* Oxford University Press, 2002.

LaMotta, Jake, Joseph Carter, and Peter Savage. *Raging Bull: My Story.* Da Capo, 1970.

Lees, Gene. *Meet Me at Jim and Andy's: Jazz Musicians and Their World.* Oxford University Press. 1988.

Mingus, Charles. *Beneath the Underdog: His World as Composed by Mingus.* Random House, 1971.

O'Malley, Terence Michael. *Black Hand/Strawman: The History of Organized Crime in Kansas City.* 2011.

Ouseley, William. *Open City: True Story of the KC Crime Family 1900–1950.* Leathers Publishing, 2008.

Porrello, Rick. *To Kill the Irishman: The War That Crippled the Mafia.* Next Hat Press, 1998.

Russell, Ross. *Bird Lives! The High Life and Hard Times of Charlie (Yardbird) Parker.* Charterhouse, 1973.

Shipton, Alyn. *Groovin High: The Life of Dizzy Gillespie.* Oxford University Press, 1999.

Smith, William Oscar. *Sideman: The Long Gig of W. O. Smith—A Memoir.* Rutledge Hill Press, 1991.

Sudhalter, Richard M. *Stardust Melody: The Life and Music of Hoagy Carmichael.* Oxford University Press, 2002.

Szwed, John F. *Jazz 101: A Complete Guide to Learning and Loving Jazz.* Hyperion Press, 2000.

———. *So What: The Life of Miles Davis.* Simon and Schuster, 2002.

Ward, Geoffrey C., and Ken Burns. *Jazz: A History of America's Music.* Alfred A. Knopf, 2000.

Whitehead, Kevin. *Why Jazz? A Concise Guide.* Oxford University Press, 2011.

ARTICLES

Cassidy, Robert. "The Blinky Palermo Story: When Gangsters Ran Boxing." *Ring* Magazine, November 1996.

"Dealer Is Found Dead in Home." *Philadelphia Enquirer,* April 15, 1949.

Feather, Leonard. "Levey Marches to a Different Drummer." *Los Angeles Times,* May 14, 1989.

———. "Photographer Levey: Forgotten Man of Jazz." Schenectady Gazette, May 18, 1988.

Fish, Scott K. "John Von Ohlon." *Modern Drummer,* March 1985.

"Four Stablemates in Olympia Bouts." *Philadelphia Enquirer,* January 4, 1944.

Gallagher, Paul. "Stan Getz on Jazz, Drugs and Robbery: 'I'm Sorry for the Crazy Thing I Did.'" *Dangerous Minds* (blog). http://dangerousminds.net/comments/stan_getz_jazz_drugs_and_robbery.

Jack, Gordon. "Stan Levey." *Jazz Journal International,* September 1999.

Korall, Burt. "Stan Levey, Bop Pioneer." *Modern Drummer,* May 1987.

Kreiswirth, Sandra. "Hot to Bop." *Daily Breeze,* May 23, 2001.

Loverro, Thom. "FBI suspected iconic 1964 Ali-Liston fight was rigged by mob." *Washington Times,* February 24, 2014.

"Mr. Carbo & His Pals." *Time,* vol. 73, issue 24, June 15, 1959.

"Phila. Fighter Fatally Hurt." *Philadelphia Enquirer,* August 17, 1947.

Riess, Steven. "Only the Ring Was Square: Frankie Carbo and the Underworld Control of American Boxing." *International Journal of the History of Sport,* 1987.

"Runyon Without Romance." *Time,* vol. 76, issue 26, December 19, 1960.

Tynan, John. "Stan the Man." *Downbeat,* March 20, 1958.

"Walker Trains in Summit Site." *Philadelphia Enquirer,* September 14, 1942.

LINER NOTES

Baker, Chet, and Art Pepper. *The Route.* Capitol Records, 1989, compact disc. Liner notes by Michael Cuscuna.

Ben Webster Quintet. *Soulville.* Verve Records, 1957, LP. Liner notes by Nat Hentoff.

Getz, Stan. *The Steamer.* Verve Records, 1957, LP. Liner notes by Greg Fishman and Bill Simon.

Hawes, Hampton. *The Sermon.* Contemporary Records, 1987, compact disc. Recorded in 1958. Liner notes by Mike Davis.

Longo, Mike. *Matrix.* Mainstream Records, 1972, LP. Liner notes by Michael Cuscuna.

Rosolino, Frank. *Free For All.* Specialty Records, 1986, LP. Recorded in 1958. Liner notes by Leonard Feather.

Stan Levey Quintet. *Stan Levey Quintet.* Mode Records, 1957, LP. Liner notes by James Rozzi and Joe Quinn.

VIDEOS

Eastwood, Clint, Billy Crystal, Jack Sheldon, Merv Griffin, and Chris Botti. *Trying to Get Good: The Jazz Odyssey of Jack Sheldon.* Directed by Penny Peyser and Doug McIntyre. Bialystock & Bloom/February Films, 2008. DVD.

Levey, Stan. *Stan Levey: "The Original Original."* Directed by Arthur Shelby Pritz. StanArt Productions, 2004. DVD.

Rumsey, Howard, and Bud Shank. *Jazz on the West Coast: The Lighthouse.* Directed by Ken Koenig. RoseKing Productions, 2006. DVD.

OTHER INTERVIEWS AND UNPUBLISHED MATERIAL

Levey, Stan. Interview by Alex Cline. Beyond Central series. University of California, Los Angeles Oral History Program, 2003.

Levey, Stan. Interview by Steve Vole. Liverpool Radio, 2001.

Levey, Stan, and Phil Abbott. "Notes of a Different Drummer." Unpublished treatment.

Levey, Stan, and Richard Clayman. "Beating the Odds." Unpublished treatment, 2001.

INDEX

Acea, Johnny, 26
Addams Family, The, 144
Adventures of Ozzie and Harriet, The, 11
"Africa," 205
Albany, Joe, 63
American Hotel, 86
Amityville Horror, The, 146
Ammons, Gene, 43, 209
Amsterdam, Morey, 164
"Angel Cake," 175
Anslinger, Harry J., 96, 103–106, 144–145, 186, 193–194, 203
Armstrong, Louis, 65–66, 76, 113
Around the World in Eighty Days, 210
Arrival of Victor Feldman, The, 190–191
Artistry Records, 170
Auld, Georgie, 48, 73
Axelrod, David, 189

Bacharach, Burt, 154
Bagley, Don, **xiii**, 170
Bailey, Colin, 175
Baker, Chet, 178, 193
Bankhead, Tallulah, 67
Barrere, Paul, 155
Basie, William James "Count," 12, 36, 42, 66, 99, 134
Basin Street East, 134
Basin Street East Proudly Presents Miss Peggy Lee, 134
Batman, 72, 144
Battle, Roy, 70
Bauer, Billy, 72
Beach Boys, 129, 140

"Bebop," 191
Bellson, Louie, 159, 167
Ben Webster Quintet, 181
Bennett, Max, 132–134, 148, 172, 194–195
Benny, Jack, 137
Benson, George, 153
Berg, Billy, 75, 78–79, 180, 195, 209
Berg, Stu, 159
Best, Denzil, 43
Bethlehem Records, 7, 132, 170–172, 174–175, 194
Bewitched, 144
Bigard, Barney, 46, 55
Bill Harris and Friends, 185
Birdland, 86–87, 91, 111–112, 196, 208
Birth of the Cool, 117
Bishop, Walter, Jr., 96
Black and White label, 47
Black Hawk Club, 205
Blaine, Hal, 126
Blakey, Art, 43, 80, 208
Blue Note Records, 197
Bolling Air Force Base, 102
Boone, Pat, 141
Boss City, 155
Bouradi, Sam, 23
Boxing Managers Guild, 33
Boyd, Nelson, 97
Brando, Marlon, 124, 127
Breaking In, 155
Britt, Stan, 174
Brown, Clifford, 120, 206
Brown, Jeannie, 155

Brown, Jumbo, 29
Brown, Lou, 191
Brown, Ray, 75, 78–79, 169, 179, 180–182, 196, 207
Brubeck, Dave, 129, 139
Budwig, Monty, 184
Bullitt, 146
Burgess, Bob, 108, 170
Burns, Ken, 158
Burns, Ralph, 73
Burton, Gary, 146–147
Butler, Frank, 124
Byas, Don, 63, 169

Calloway, Cab, 24, 54–55
Camarillo State Mental Hospital, 80, 82
Candoli, Conte, **xviii**, 72, 100, 124–125, 146, 170–172, 174–176, 183–184, 196
Candoli, Pete, 72
Capitol Records, 134, 159
Capone, Al, 55, 72
Carbo, Frankie, 33–34, 46
Carlton, Larry, 153, 195
Carmichael, Hoagy, Jr., 46, 155
Carson, Johnny, 144, 157
Carter, Benny, 74
Casino Royale, 95
Catalano, Joseph, 86
Cataldo, Adele, 88, 93, 103, 135–136
Catlett, Sid, 74, 169
Central Avenue, 172
Cerra, Steven, 126
Charles, Ezzard, 24
Charles, Ray, 134, 146

Charlie Parker with Strings, 112
Charmichael, Hoagy, Jr., 122
Cherry, Don, 124
Childress, Buddy, 170
"Chrisdee," 188
Christy, June, **xi–xii**, 127, 170
Cincinnati Kid, The, 146
City of Glass, 106
Clark, Sonny, **xxiii**, 124, 175–176, 197
Clarke, Stanley, 204
Classic Records, 169
Claude Thornhill Orchestra, 118
Clicquot Club Eskimos, 11
Clift, Montgomery, 139
Clinton, Bill, 164
Clyde, Red, 170–171
Coasters, 154
Coburn, James, 124, 144
Cohn, Al, 72
Cole, Nat King, 109, 119, 133
Coleman, Ornette, 124, 205
Collette, Buddy, 78
Collins, Jimmy, 23
Coltrane, John, 30, 86, 155
"Compared to What," 189
Concert by the Sea, 198
Concerts by the Sea, 207
"Confessin' the Blues," 53
"Confirmation," 67
Contemporary Records, 7, 176, 186, 190
Cool Hand Luke, 146
Cooper, Bob, **xiv**, 124, 127, 167, 172, 176, 183
Cottler, Irv, 157
"Cottontail," 65

Count Basie Orchestra, 66
Court and Spark, 194
Curtis, Tony, 137
Cyprus Hill, 155

Darin, Bobby, 140, 164
Dave Brubeck Quartet, 139
Davis, Bette, 164
Davis, Mike, 186
Davis, Miles, **iii**, 42–43, 67–70, 85, 87, 97, 117–118, 120, 153, 174, 181, 186, 191, 197, 205, 207–208
de Koenigswarter, Pannonica, 113
De La Soul, 155
Decca Records, 53
"Deep Gully," 155
DeFranco, Buddy, 30
Del Coronado Hotel, 137
Dempsey, Jack, 31
Dennis, Don, **xi**, 170
Dial Records, 79, 114, 169
Disneyland, 131
Dizzy Gillespie 1945–1946, 169
Donte's Jazz Supper Club, 198
Dorham, Kenny, 96
Downbeat Club, 24, 27, 30, 49, 55, 96, 144
Downbeat magazine, 188
Downtown House, 77–78
Drake Hotel, 78
Drummin' the Blues, **xxii**, 183
Dubrow, Kevin, 154
Dundee, Angelo, 33
Durante, Jimmy, 145
Dylan, Bob, 126

Eager, Allen, **v**, 87
Earl Hines Band, 54
Earle Theater, 11, 19, 20, 26–28, 30, 39

Eastwood, Clint, 158, 198
Eckstine, Billy, 43, 55
Eldridge, Roy, 24, 59, 202
Ellington, Duke, 42, 46, 118, 129, 190
Ellis, Herb, 30, 179, 181
Ellison, Ralph, 61, 65, 113
European Tour 1953, The, 170
Evans, Bill, 191, 204
Evans, Gil, 117–118

Fadis, John, 196
Fahrenheit, 205
Fantasy Records, 185
Feather, Leonard, 47, 59, 61, 158, 207
Feldman, Marilyn, 197–198
Feldman, Victor, **xxi**, 124, 164, 167, 188, 190–191, 197–198
Ferguson, Maynard, 100
Ferina, Tony, 170
Festival of Modern American Jazz, **xiii**, 109
"Fever," 133–134, 147
Fifty-Second Street, **xxx**, 39, 41–42, 45–48, 51, 55, 63–64, 71, 80, 86, 111, 137, 181, 183
Finney, John, 23
Fitzgerald, Ella, 12, 42, 98, 134, 137–140, 143, 184, 204
For Musicians Only, 179–180
Fox, Tim, 165
Frazier, Joe, 31
Free For All, 188–189, 207
Freeman, Russ, 146
Fulmer, Gene, 46

Gaillard, Slim, 78
Galbraith, Barry, **xiii**, 170

Gardner, Ava, 79, 128

Garland, Red, 97

Garment, Lenny, 48–49, 159–160, 202

Garner, Erroll, 48, 97, 109, 198

Gaskin, Leonard, **ii–iii,** 68

George Shearing Trio, 48

Gershwin, George, 210

Getz Meets Mulligan in Hi-Fi, 182

Getz, Stan, **xvii,** 72, 85–86, 129, 177, 179–180, 182, 184, 198–200, 203

Giancana, Sam, 137–138

Giardello, Joey, 31

Gibbs, Terry, 85, 146, 167

Gibson, Harry "The Hipster," 78

Gilgore, Jerry, 25

Gillespie, Dizzy, **xii, xx,** 7, 24–27, 29–30, 39, 42–45, 47–49, 52, 54–55, 59, 61–62, 66–68, 71–80, 96, 98–99, 109–110, 113–114, 119–120, 167, 169, 179, 180, 191, 196, 199, 200, 207

Gillespie, Lorraine, **xii,** 66, 199

Giuffre, Jimmy, 124, 172

Goodman, Benny, 12, 27–29, 71, 73, 131, 172, 205, 208

Goodman, Irving, 29

Goodman, Marv, 22

Gordon, Dexter, **iii, xviii,** 43, 68, 69, 70, 83, 120, 154, 174–175, 177, 197, 200, 207

Graettinger, Bob, 106

Grand Stan, 175

Grand Terrace Ballroom, 55, 72

Grant, Cary, 134

Granz, Norman, 82–83, 138, 179–180, 182

Grateful Dead, 99, 202

Green, Johnny, 50

Greenspan, Alan, 48–49

Griffin, Merv, 147

Guaraldi, Vince, **xvi**

Guerin, John, 155, 195

Guild Records, 74, 114

Guthrie, Arlo, 194

Haddix, Chuck, 63

Haden, Charlie, 124, 146

Haig, Al, 59, 61, 63, 67, 75, 78, 85, 169, 196, 200–201

Hancock, Herbie, 205

Handy, George, 169

Harris, Benny, 43, 62

Harris, Bill, 19, 72, 185

Harris, Eddie, 188

Hart, Clyde, 158

Hawes, Hampton, 79, 146, 186–187, 201

Hawkins, Coleman, 43–44, 55, 59, 207

Hawkins, Erskine, 11

Heath Brothers, 30

Hefti, Neal, 72–73, 144

Henderson, Skitch, 144

Hentoff, Nat, 181

Herman, Woody, 71–74, 77, 114, 125, 184–185, 201–202

Hines, Earl, 54–55, 72

Hissing of Summer Lawns, The, 194

"Hit That Thing," 175

Hofberg, Jack, 23

Hoffman, Mary, 13, 93, 103

"Hold the Line," 166

Holiday, Billie, 69–70, 87, 105, 138, 194

Holman, Bill, 100–101, 109, 170, 172

Homey, 155

Hoover, J. Edgar, 103–104

Horowitz, Vladimir, 210

Hosfield, Johnny, 43

"Hot House," 67

Hot Rats, 194

Hotel Pennsylvania, 71

Howard Theater, 96

Howe, Bones, 171

Hudson, Rock, 128

I Dream of Jeannie, 144

"I Love Being Here with You," 134

"I'm a Woman," 133

Intervention Band, 165

Ives, Burl, 98

Jack Sheldon: Live at Don Mupo's Gold Nugget, 148

Jackson, Chubby, 72

Jackson, Michael, 205

Jackson, Milt, 75, 169, 196

Jagger, Mick, 164

Jazz at the Philharmonic, 82

Jazz: A History of America's Music, 158

Jennings, Bob, 23

Jerome, Henry, 48

Johnny P. and the Wiseguys, 166

Johnson, J. J., 117

Johnson, Jack, 68

Jolly, Pete, 178

Jones, Davy, 154

Jones, Gus, 23

Jones, Hank, 47, 56, 63, 137

Jones, Jennifer, 79

Jones, Jimmy, 83

Jones, Jo, 36

Jones, Philly Joe, 30

Jones, Quincy, **xxx,** 42, 60, 134, 153

Jordan, Duke, 83

Kamuca, Joan, **v**

Kamuca, Jonie, **v**

Kamuca, Richie, **v,** 97–98, 175, 178, 184, 202
Kane, Dick, 31–32
Keepnews, Peter, 164
Keltner, Jim, 125–126, 163
Kennedy, John F., 136–138, 201
Kennedy, Kathleen, 147
Kenton, Stan, **ix–xiii,** 8, 99–103, 106–109, 112, 119, 170, 202–203, 205
Kerouac, Jack, 87, 208
Kessel, Barney, 83
Kind of Blue, 181
Kirk, Roland, 170
Kluger, Irv, 45
Konitz, Lee, 99, 101, 110, 117–118, 170
Korall, Burt, 170
Kotick, Teddy, 96
Kreibich, Paul, 196
Krupa, Gene, 12, 19, 129

LaFaro, Scott, 190–191, 203–204
Lamond, Don, 183
Land, Harold, 124, 188
Landau, Mike, 153
Laredo, 144
Lay, Dorsey, 23
Led Zeppelin, 195
Lee, Peggy, 131–134, 136, 138, 140, 147, 184, 194, 204
Lees, Gene, 125
Leigh, Janet, 137
Leroy Vinnegar Jazz Institute, 210
Leshin, Phil, 74
Levey, Angela, **v–vi,** **xviii, xxix,** 16, 45, 87–89, 92–95, 98, 102–103, 106, 108, 111–113, 119, 120–122, 125, 127, 135–137, 143, 147, 151–152, 155–157,

159, 162, 164–165, 170, 173, 180, 190, 195–198, 204, 207–208, 210
Levey, Anthony, 165
Levey, Christopher, **xx,** **xxiv, xxv,** 121, 148, 151–155, 158, 162, 164, 166, 188, 200, 205
Levey, Danny, 166
Levey, David, Sr., 10, 13–24, 32–33, 88–89
Levey, David, Jr., **xxv,** 89, 121, 128, 134, 140–141, 151, 153–155, 157, 162, 164, 166, 188, 190, 202, 205, 211
Levey, Erica, 166
Levey, Essie, **i,** 9–11, 14, 16, 18–19, 26–28, 32, 41, 92–93, 103, 135–136, 164
Levey, Joan, 89
Levey, Joseph, 165
Levey, Kate, 166
Levey, Kristen, 165
Levey, Robert, **xxv,** 84, 103, 121, 140, 146, 153, 155, 164–165, 205, 210
Levey, Suzanna, 166
Levey, Tara, 166
Levine, John, 120
Levy, Diane, **xxiv**
Levy, Irving, 86–87, 112
Levy, Lou, **xxiv,** 132, 134, 174, 177, 182, 184
Levy, Morris, 86, 87, 112
Lewis, Jerry, 121
Lewis, John, 179–180
Lewis, Mel, 126, 133
Liberace, 124, 164
Liberty Records, 183
Lighthouse All-Stars, **xxi, xxiii,** 120, 122–125, 127, 129, 153, 155, 176, 183, 190,

195, 197, 204, 207
Lighthouse Club, **xiv–xv, xxi, xxiii,** 119–127, 129, 153, 155, 176, 183, 195–197, 200, 204, 206–207
Little Feat, 155
Livingston, Edwin, 196
London, Julie, 164
"Long Island Sound," 85
Longo, Mike, 199
Los Angeles Jazz Institute, 196
Los Angeles Mirror, 127
Louis, Joe, 35, 87
"Love Me or Levey," 176
"Lover Come Back to Me," 184
Luciano, Lucky, 104, 144–145
Ludwig, **vii,** 100–101
Lukather, Steve, 153, 205
Lynch, Bill, 158–159

M*A*S*H, 48
Madison Square Garden, 12, 35, 137
Man with the Golden Arm, The, 84
Mancini, Henry, 144
Mandel, Johnny, 48
Manne, Florence "Flip," 119
Manne, Shelly, **xxii,** 45, 71, 83, 119, 123, 126, 177, 202, 205–206
Mannix, 149
Marionette Hotel, 57
Marquette, Pee Wee, 87
Marsalis, Wynton, 160
Marshall, Frank, 147
Marshall, Jack, 147
Martin Band Instrument Company, **xxvi,** 128
Marvin, Lee, 124
McCann, Les, 188
McGhee, Howard, 66, 79

McPherson, Charles, 196
McQueen, Steve, 146
McShann, Jay "Hootie," 36, 51–53, 55, 158
Memorial Auditorium, 50
Meredith, Burgess, 67
Middlebrooks, Wilfred, 138
Miller, Georgie, 20–22
Millinder, Lucky, 52–53
Mingus, Charles, 79, 170
Minichiello, Ziggy, 170
Minton's Playhouse, 63, 112
Mission: Impossible, 146, 149
"Misty," 198
Mitchell, Joni, 132, 191, 194–195
Mitchell, Red, 185
Mode Records, 184
Mondragon, Joe, 147
Monk, Thelonious, 43–44, 56, 87, 207
Monkees, 154
Monroe, Marilyn, 128, 137–138
Montgomery, Bob, 17, 32
Moon, Keith, 170
Morello, Joe, 139–140
Morgenstern, Dan, 114
Morte, George, 106
Motion, Paul, 191
Mulligan, Gerry, 100–102, 117–118, 182, 202
Munsters, The, 144, 147
Music for Lighthouse-keeping, 176

Nanny, The, 162
New York Times, 164
Newport Jazz Festival, 203
Nixon, Richard, 48, 159, 160
Norman, Gene, 129

Ode to a Highflying Bird, 211
Olympic Fight Club, 17
On the Road, 87
Onyx Club, 44, 46, 60
Outlaw Blues Band, 155

Pacific Jazz Records, 178
Page, "Hot Lips," 36, 64
Paich, David, 153
Paich, Marty, 124, 153
Paint Your Wagon, 148
Palermo, Frank "Blinky," 33–34, 46
Paramount Theater, 29
Parker, Charlie "Bird," ii–iv, xiii, 7, 36–37, 42, 48, 51–69, 73–80, 82–83, 85–86, 95–96, 99, 104–105, 109–115, 118–119, 140–141, 146, 158, 160, 163, 169, 174, 180, 182, 186, 193–194, 196, 199, 200, 208–209, 211
Parker, Leo, 80
Pasadena Civic Center, 129
"Peace Train," 194
Peck, Gregory, 128
Pepper, Art, 154, 178
Perkins, Bill, **xxi**, 183
Pete Kelly's Blues, 134
Peterson, Leo, 23
Peterson, Oscar, 47, 177, 181
Pettiford, Oscar, 43–44, 48, 170, 206
Phillips, Flip, 72
Pierce, John, 153
Pinnick, Chris, 154
Play Misty for Me, 198
Playboy, 181
Porcaro, Jeff, 153
Porcaro, Joe, 153
Porcaro, Steve, 153
Potter, Tommy, 83
Powell, Bud, 68, 87, 175

Powell, Gordon "Specs," 42
Presley, Elvis, 136
Prestige Records, 85
Previn, André, 144
Pritz, Arthur, 89
Private Reserve, 195

Quiet Riot, 154

Rachmaninoff, Sergei, 210
Raeburn, Boyd, 73, 158
Ramey, Gene, 36–37, 53, 64, 85
Ranier, Tom, 196
Reagan, Ronald, 194, 210
Redman, Joshua, 160
Regal Drumsticks, 101
Reman Scott Studios, 47
Rendezvous Club, 96
Rich, Buddy, **xxvi**, 19, 128–129, 156–157, 202
Richards, Emil, 143
Richards, Keith, 164
Riddle, Nelson, 137, 144–145
Rivers, Larry, 48–49
Riviera Hotel and Casino, 136
Roach, Max, **xxii**, 44–45, 68, 71, 74, 119–120, 123, 129, 183, 206
Roberts, Howard, 147
Robinson, Eddie, 44
Robinson, Sugar Ray, 46, 68–69, 86, 97
Rodney, Mark, 155
Rodney, Red, 30, 83, 155
Rogers, Shorty, 143, 178
Rolling Stones, **xxxii**, 7, 126, 163, 211
Rooney, Mickey, 79
"Rosanna," 205
Rosemary's Baby, 151

Rosolino, Frank, **v, xi, xviii, xxi, xxiii,** 100–101, 107, 124–125, 170, 174–176, 183, 188–189, 206–207
Rosolino, Jean, 125, 206
Ross, Diana, 194
Round Midnight, 200
Route, The, 178
Rowels, Jimmy, 185
Rowland, Gene, 103
Royal, Ernie, **x,** 108
Royal Roost, 88
Rubinstein, Arthur, 210
Rude Awakening, 162
Rugolo, Pete, 127
Rumsey, Howard, **xiv, xxi,** 120, 122–124, 176, 183, 207
Rumsey, Joyce, 120
Russell, Curly, **v,** 59, 63, 67–68, 75, 80, 85, 207–208
Russell, Ross, 79
Russo, Bill, **xiii,** 100, 109, 170

Saint Dominic's Preview, 188
Saks, Sol, 147
"Salt Peanuts," 25, 66, 78
Saunders, Jackie, 23
Savoy Ballroom, 12, 52
Scaggs, Boz, 153
Schifrin, Lalo, **xxx,** 144, 146, 149
Schildkraut, Davey, 170
Schoolhouse Rock!, 147
Scott, Tom, 195
"Scrapple from the Apple," 182
Sermon, The, 186–187, 201
"Shadow of Your Smile, The," 48
Shank, Bud, **xiv,** 124, 183
Shaw, Artie, 19
"Shaw 'Nuff," 67

Shearing, George, 48, 146
Sheldon, Jack, **xiv,** 147–148
Shelly's Manne Hole, 205
Sherman Hotel, 83
Shoemake, Charlie, 196, 200
Shoemake, Sandi, 196
Shorter, Wayne, 205
Showboat Club, 97
Shreve, Dick, 183
Shrine Auditorium, **xiii**
Siegel, Nat, 26
Simone, Nina, 170
Sims, Zoot, **xi,** 27, 72, 99, 101, 170, 172–173, 175, 208
Sinatra, Frank, 67, 84, 121, 137, 144–146, 157
Sinatra, Spencer, 93–94
Six Feet Under, 162
Slack, Freddie, 73
Smiley, Bill, 170
Smith, Don, 170
Smith, Newton, 23
Smith, Oscar, 26, 186
Smith, Paul, 138–139, 141
Smothers Brothers, 124
Soldier Meyers', 85
Soultone Cymbals, 165
Soulville, 181
Specialty Records, 188
Specter, Phil, 99
Spielberg, Steven, 147
Spotlite Club, **ii–iii,** 60, 68–69, 80, 174
Spring Garden Gym, 20, 26, 186
Stan Getz Quartet, 177
Stan Kenton Orchestra, **ix–xiii,** 8, 94, 99–103, 105–110, 112, 117, 119–120, 124–126, 132, 143, 147, 170, 195, 203

Stan Levey Plays the Compositions of Bill Holman, Bob Cooper, and Jimmy Giuffre, 172
Stan Levey Quintet, 184
Stan Levey: The Original Original, 89
"Stanley the Steamer," 174
Stanley the Steamer, 174
Staples Center, 164
Steamer, The, 177
Steel Pier, 103, 105
Steely Dan, 153, 191
Steve Allen Show, The, 128
Stevens, Cat, 194
Stewart, Teddy, 80
Stillman's Gym, 69
Stitt, Sonny, 80, 91, 97–98, 179–180, 186, 208–209
Stoller, Alvin, 157
Strayhorn, Billy, 112
Streisand, Barbra, 148–149
Sunnyside Gardens, 49
Supremes, 140
Swiss Movement, 188
Szwed, John F., 106

Tate, Buddy, 66
Tate, Flip, 43
Tatum, Art, 11, 47–48, 209–210
Taylor, Elizabeth, 67
Ted Burke's Music Store, 18
Temple Youth Club, 22
"There'll Never Be Another You," 177
Thiele, Bob, 155
Thirtysomething, 162
"This Time the Drum's On Me," 174
This Time the Drum's On Me, 174, 200
Thomas, Joe, 48
Thomas, Willie, 23

Thompson, Lucky, 76, 169
Three Deuces Club, **v**, 42, 60, 66–68, 71, 74, 87
Thriller, 205
"Thundering Herd," 72
Tick Tock Club, 43
Tin Pan Alley, 74, 112
Tollin, Ellis, **ii**, 41, 43, 47, 100, 155
Tomez, Pedro, 23
Tomkins, Les, 209
Tonight Show Band, *The*, 196
Tonight Show, The, 128, 144, 196
Toto, 153–154, 166, 205
Tough, Dave, 45, 71, 73
Travis, Nick, 30
Trident restaurant, 147
Trinity Broadcasting Studio, 79
Tristano, Lennie, 113
True Lies, 162
Truman, Harry S., 104
Tunney, Gene, 31
Turner, Big Joe, 36
Turner's Arena, 81
Twentieth Century Fox, 144
Twenty-One Saxophone Salute, 114
Tyler, Ben, 50

Universal Studios, 144

Valley Arena, 49
Van Dyke, Shirley, 84–85, 121, 146, 210
Van Morrison, 188
Vaughan, Sarah, 42–43, 69, 83, 98, 109, 119
Ventura, Charlie, 73
Verse Records, 175
Verve Records, 177, 179, 181–182
Vines, Ziggy, 158

Vinnegar, Kevin, 155
Vinnegar, Leroy, 155, 174–175, 177–178, 186, 188, 210
Vinnegar, Mark, 155

Waits, Tom, 147, 191, 205
Walker, Johnny, 23–24
Wallington, George, **v**, 68, 85, 87
Warwick, Carl, 39
Warwick, Dionne, 154
Watson, Bobby, 114
Watts, Charlie, **xxxii**, 7, 163–164, 190, 211
Watts, Shirley, 211
Wayne, Chuck, 48
We Insist! Max Roach's Freedom Now Suite, 206
Webb, Chick, 11–12, 52, 138
Webster, Ben, 36, 42, 64–65, 181, 185
Webster, Freddie, 69–70
West Coast Jazz, 177
West Coasting, 172
West, Harold "Doc," 67
"West Side Story Medley," 128
Whitaker, Forest, 158
Whitehead, Kevin, 60
Widra, Joe, 96–97
Williams, Cootie, 113
Williams, Dick, 127
Williams, Ike, 17, 32, 50
Williams, Martin, 60
Williams, Mary Lou, 35
Williamson, Claude, 172
Wilson, Brian, 140
Wilson, Shadow, 25, 97
Wilson, Teddy, 210
Winding, Kai, 85
Witherspoon, Tim, 31

Young, Lester, 36, 42, 64, 83

Zappa, Frank, 132, 191, 194
Zildjian, 100, 109
"Zoot," 107, 170